The John Experiment

How John's Gospel can
help you know Jesus better

by
Andrew Page

VTR
Publications

ISBN 978-3-95776-070-8

Author photo on the back cover:
(c) Roger Eldridge Photography, www.eldridgephotos.com

Cover design: Chris Allcock

Contents

Acknowledgements

I am grateful to Chris Allcock for his willingness, once again, to do the drawings and the cover design, and especially to Thomas Mayer for agreeing to publish this book.

A number of people read the manuscript and gave me their comments and suggestions, so I am glad to thank them here: John Ayrton, Sanjay Mall, Rosemary Pepper, Biddy Taylor, Charlie Watkins and Wolfgang Widmann.

I owe a huge debt to friends, many of them in Above Bar Church Southampton, who pray for me and encourage me. I would be a lesser person without my church family.

I am more excited by John's Gospel than ever before! As I have learnt to meditate my way through this Gospel my love for Jesus has grown, along with my desire to tell others about him. I pray that many people will make the same discovery.

To God be the glory!

Andrew Page
andrew@themarkdrama.com

My Introduction:
Invitation to an Experiment

This is a book about two things at once.

First, it's about learning the Gospel of John. I don't think John originally wrote his book to be read but to be listened to: few people in the first century could have expected to own a copy for themselves. John wrote it so people could memorize it. Not word for word, but bit by bit – so they could get to know Jesus better and tell the story to others.

So, second, this is a book about rediscovering Jesus. You may already know John's Gospel very well, or you may just be starting out: but as we spend time together in his book the aim will be that as a result we will admire, love and enjoy Jesus more. If that's what you want, you're in the right place.

So that's what the experiment is about: learning the Gospel so we can get to know Jesus better. I hope you will try it out for yourself.

Please take time to read the rest of this introduction. It won't take you long, but it will help you get the maximum out of *The John Experiment*.

The Structure of John's Gospel

After an introduction, which is the whole of chapter 1, I think John has divided the story he wants to tell into six main sections.

Each of the sections consists of two signs and three blocks, and there's a logic to how they fit together.

Look, for example, at Section Two, which runs from John 4:43 to 5:47. Here is the structure as I see it:

Two signs

A. Jesus heals a royal official's son (4:43-54)
B. Jesus heals a paralysed man (5:1-15)

Three blocks

X. The claim (5:16-30)
Y. The evidence (5:31-40)
Z. The diagnosis (5:41-47)

There are five things to notice about this structure:

1. The two signs reveal something about Jesus

In this case they show his power and authority, prompting the question *Who is this man?* Most of the signs in this Gospel (though not all of them) are miracles Jesus performs, but they are always signposts pointing us to him.

Every one of the six sections has two signs; usually, as here, the two signs are at the beginning of their section.

2. The three blocks explain what the signs reveal

In Section Two, the fact that Jesus has healed a man on the Sabbath has provoked strong opposition from the religious leaders.

So in the three blocks Jesus states his *claim* to be in unique relationship with God the Father, provides *evidence* for the truth of this, and gives his own *diagnosis* of the condition of the religious leaders' hearts.

And all the sections have three blocks of material which explain what the signs reveal.

3. The whole section has a main theme

The theme of Section Two is The Authority. The signs show Jesus' authority in two healing miracles, while in the blocks we hear Jesus explaining where his authority comes from.

And every one of the six sections has its own theme.

4. I have given each sign and each block sub-headings

Let me explain what I mean. Some of the sections cover a number of chapters in John's Gospel, which means the signs and blocks are rather long.

So, in order to help us grasp their message I have added sub-headings. For example, here are my sub-headings for both of Section Two's signs:

A. Jesus heals a royal official's son (4:43-54)

    1. Great need (46-47)
    2. Effortless authority (48-50a)
    3. Growing faith (50b-54)

B. Jesus heals a paralysed man (5:1-15)

1. Great need (1-3)
2. Effortless authority (5-9a)
3. Growing opposition (9b-15)

And I have done the same thing for the three blocks.

If you don't like my sub-headings I have no problem with that: feel free to find some which work better for you. But sub-headings, especially in the longer signs and the longer blocks, will help us to get hold of the meaning.

(For the complete outline of my structure of John's Gospel, see Appendix 3.)

5. The section can easily be learnt by heart

This is not about learning every word, but simply the order of the events (with the sub-headings) in the section. I have tested this: most people can do this in 10 minutes. And that's true of all the sections.

But why should I learn John by heart?

That's a great question. But there are some very good reasons:

I.   Because the Bible is the word of God it has remarkable power. We often forget this. In Psalm 119:11 David says to God: *I have hidden your word in my heart that I might not sin against you.*

II.   Because John has written his Gospel to make this easy. If you read *The John Experiment* you will notice how the structure of the Gospel makes learning it very easy. My guess is that the Holy Spirit led John to write this way because he wants us to have his word in our hearts.

III.   Because learning the Gospel in this way makes it possible to do Bible study in the shower without getting your Bible wet! Of course I normally have my Bible with me when I am doing Bible study, but sometimes it's brilliant to meditate on the Bible just using your memory. So as you are walking down the road you can tell yourself the Gospel events and begin talking to Jesus about what you are remembering.

IV.   Because I would love you to experience what I have experienced. I have enjoyed this Gospel for decades, but only in the last few years have I been able to meditate my way through John. The Holy Spirit has used this to help me experience Jesus more. And this makes me want to share this with others.

How to use this book

This book is like a basic commentary, but one you can read through instead of just using for reference. As we look at the six main sections of John there'll be an introduction called *Enjoying the View*: this provides the structure and the main theme of the section.

Next comes *Unpacking the Content*. Here I look at each part of the section in turn, explaining the message and showing how the two signs and the three blocks are linked to each other.

Then I make some suggestions as to how you could memorize the section (this is called *Learning the Gospel*). Most people aren't used to learning by heart, but it really is worth it. And remember we're not talking about learning every word but the order of events (with the sub-headings) in the section. As I mentioned above, most people can do this in 10 minutes.

One good way of getting the learning done is to team up with a friend. You agree to both read through, say, Section One and learn the order of events. Then you meet up to go for a walk or have a coffee, and re-tell the section together (see My Conclusion, point 3, page 128, for more details). Doing this with a friend will help you to do the learning rather than just skip it!

The last part is called *Meeting the Lord*. This is a reminder of the reason we are doing all this: we want to rediscover Jesus. As you talk to the Lord about what you have been reading you will start knowing, admiring and loving him more.

Please don't read *The John Experiment* too quickly! You might want to take a week over each of the six sections, so that you have time to let what you are reading sink in. You might want to meet up with a friend once a week who is also trying the John experiment, to tell one another the stories and to talk about Jesus.

Thank you for reading my introduction; now it's time to read John's.

I am praying that everyone who reads this book will enjoy John's Gospel and enjoy meeting Jesus. The John experiment starts now...

John's Introduction (John 1:1-51)

Some introductions you can take or leave: the most you can say about them is that they are taking up space.

But John's is different. He is going to tell us the story of what happened when God came into our world as a human being. His introduction is designed to show us how Jesus transformed John himself and the other disciples, too.

And to give us hope that the same thing could happen to us.

Enjoying the View

A. Jesus: the Word of God (1:1-18)
a. The supremacy of Jesus (1-5)
b. John the Baptist and Jesus (6-8)
c. Reactions to Jesus (9-14)
b'. John the Baptist and Jesus (15)
a'. The supremacy of Jesus (16-18)

B. Jesus: who is this man? (1:19-51)
1. What Isaiah says (19-28)
2. What John says (29-34)
3. What Andrew says (35-42)
4. What Nathanael says (43-49)
5. What Jesus says (50-51)

The introduction to John's Gospel clearly has two parts. The first, usually known as the Prologue, tells us about the link between Jesus and God, though the central paragraph already introduces the topic of how people react to him.

This is the focus of part B of John's Introduction. When people responded positively to Jesus, why was this? *Who did they think he was?*

It would be good to read through John's Introduction before reading further. During the first part you may find yourself worshipping; the second part gives us the opportunity to ask ourselves a question: *Who is this man?*

Unpacking the Content

A. Jesus: the Word of God (1-18)

This astonishing passage has mirror links. This means that a and a' have something in common and b and b' have something in common. It's verse 15 which gives the game away: it seems so out of place that some translations even resort to putting the verse in brackets.

But it's not out of place: it's there because of the mirror links.

a. – The supremacy of Jesus (1-5)

John begins in verse 1 by talking about *the Word*. The beginning of verse 14 explains that this is a name for Jesus: *The Word became flesh and made his dwelling among us* (14a).

Jews in the first century knew that God had created everything by his word. In the psalms we read: *By the word of the Lord the heavens were made, their starry host by the breath of his mouth. For he spoke, and it came to be; he commanded, and it stood firm* (Ps 33:6,9; see also Gen 1:3ff).

John tells us that Jesus was in relationship with God (see 1-2), but he goes even further: the Word *was* God (1). He confirms this by adding that Jesus was involved with God in the process of creation: *through him all things were made* (3a).

Human beings have a relationship with Jesus too: *In him was life, and that life was the light of all mankind* (4). Whenever any of us starts understanding anything about the purpose of our lives and the existence of our Creator, that's down to Jesus. He's giving us light.

However, something's gone wrong: *the light shines in the darkness* (5a). John hasn't finished his first paragraph yet, but he's already telling us that there's something in opposition to the light.

But we don't need to worry. The light will not be beaten: *the darkness has not overcome it* (5b). The Greek word for *overcome* means *understood*, too: so a good translation would be *the darkness has not mastered it*.

John has begun his Gospel by making it very clear that Jesus is supreme: he is God himself. He longs for us to come to the same conclusion.

b. – John the Baptist and Jesus (6-8)

John the Baptist's role is not to be the centre of attention himself, but to focus everyone's attention elsewhere: *he came only as a witness to the light* (8b). And the whole point of what John did was *so that through him all might believe* (7b). Believing in Jesus is a major theme in this book (see chapter 20:30-31).

And John the Gospel-writer wants us to know why John the Baptist came: he was *sent from God* (6) to be a signpost pointing to Jesus (see 7-8).

c. – Reactions to Jesus (9-14)

John tells us how people responded when Jesus, *the true light* (9), came into the world.

Some said No. Most people *did not recognise him* (10) and so *did not receive him* (11). This was all the more extraordinary because Jesus was involved in creating all these people (see 10), which means they owed their very existence to him.

Some said Yes. John explains what receiving Jesus means by telling us that some people *believed in his name* (12). At this stage we may not know what this involves, but we will understand it better as we move through the Gospel (and read John's explanation in chapter 20:30-31 as to why he wrote his book).

And look at the result! Those who say *Yes* to Jesus become *children of God* (12), people who are in such a close relationship with the Creator that they can call him *Father*.

And that isn't down to their family tree or their parents' decision: people who believe in Jesus are *born of God* (13). In other words, when anyone opens themselves up to the reality of Jesus, that's because God is at work in them. There is more about this in Section One of the Gospel (see chapter 3:5-7).

Now John tells us why we can be confident that it's true that *the Word became flesh and made his dwelling among us* (14a). The reason is that the apostles witnessed everything and saw the evidence: *We have seen his glory, the glory of the one and only Son, who came from the Father, full of grace and truth* (14b).

The best way of understanding that word *glory* is to think of it as the *godness* of God: it is what makes God God. In the Old Testament Moses had said to God *Show me your glory* (Exod 33:18); now John is saying to us: *Do you want to see the glory and the reality of God? Then look at Jesus!* That's why he says *We have seen his glory* (14): he's encouraging us to keep reading and to keep looking.

And to be making our own mind up as to how we are going to react to Jesus.

b' – John the Baptist and Jesus (15)

We have already seen in part b that John the Baptist's role was to be a signpost pointing to Jesus (see 7-8). That is exactly what he is doing here: *He who comes after me has surpassed me because he was before me* (15).

John is not only saying that Jesus *existed* before him, which is extraordinary enough because Jesus was born some six months after John. His message could not be clearer: Jesus is *much more important* than John the Baptist.

a' – The supremacy of Jesus (16-18)

John the Gospel-writer ends his prologue by telling us, as he did at the beginning (see part a, chapter 1:1-2), that Jesus is in relationship with God and is God himself: *No one has ever seen God, but the one and only Son, who is himself God and is in the closest relationship with the Father, has made him known* (18).

So John explains what effect meeting Jesus had on him and the other apostles: *Out of his fulness we have all received grace in place of grace already received* (16). Of course there was grace when God gave Israel the Law through Moses (see 17a), but John wants us to know that people who encounter Jesus experience *grace and truth* on a completely different level (see 17b).

That's because of who Jesus is.

It's worth mentioning here that in verse 17 John calls Jesus *Christ* for the first time. The word could also be translated *Messiah*: the man John has come to know is the Saviour-King promised in the Old Testament. And, says John, he is also the one and only Son of God (see 14).

The first eighteen verses of the Gospel introduce us to Jesus, the Word of God, who is supreme. John tells us that he is none other than God himself in human flesh (see 1,14,18), and invites us to believe in him (12, see also chapter 20:30-31).

So it is obvious what the focus is going to be in the rest of John's Introduction.

B. Jesus: who is this man? (19-51)

The second half of this first chapter consists of a conversation between John the Baptist and some religious leaders (19-28), followed by the account of how some of those who later became disciples of Jesus first encountered him (29-51).

But the issue all these elements have in common is the identity of Jesus. John has already told us *his* view; now he tells us the conclusions others reached when they met Jesus, and ends by telling us something Jesus said about himself.

1. – What Isaiah says (19-28)

It's John the Baptist speaking here, and he will quote words from the Old Testament prophet Isaiah in verse 23.

But first we see that the religious inspection party sent from Jerusalem (see 19) are curious as to who John is, especially when he says *I am not the Messiah* (20). Their two guesses are based on Old Testament prophecy: maybe John is Elijah (see Mal 4:5-6), or the Prophet-Messiah promised through Moses (see Deut 18:15,17-18).

So the question comes again: *Who are you?* (22)

This is the point at which John chooses to quote Isaiah: *I am the voice of one calling in the wilderness, 'Make straight the way for the Lord'* (23).

This is a jaw-dropping moment. By using these words John is not so much explaining who *he* is, as revealing who he is preparing the way for: *the Lord.*

In the Isaiah passage that word *Lord* is written in four capital letters (see Isa 40:3), which stands for the name of God: Yahweh. This is the name God had used when he had revealed himself to Moses from the burning bush (see Exod 3:14-15).

Do you see what John the Baptist is doing in verse 23? He is claiming to be preparing the way for Yahweh, God himself. I don't know if John fully understood what he was telling his examiners, but the message is clear: *I am preparing the way for Jesus. And Jesus is God.*

This is what Isaiah says.

Now John takes the opportunity once more to be a signpost, as he explains that the one coming after him is so great that John would not even be worthy to be his slave (see 27).

And no wonder, if Isaiah is right that the Coming One is God himself.

2. – What John says (29-34)

Now Jesus appears in person for the first time in John's Gospel, prompting John the Baptist to be a signpost again: *This is the one I meant when I said, 'A man who comes after me has surpassed me because he was before me'* (30).

We don't even know who John is talking to here: it seems like he is simply grabbing every opportunity to point people to Jesus and to his identity.

First, John says Jesus is *the Lamb of God, who takes away the sin of the world* (29). This is extraordinary.

John is either thinking of the lambs people brought to the temple in Jerusalem to be sacrificed for their sins or of the Passover lambs who died so that the Israelites could escape God's judgment. *This* lamb Jesus, says John, is provided by God, and his death will deal with the sins of the whole world (see 29).

And second, Jesus is *God's Chosen One* (34). What has convinced John of this, is seeing the Holy Spirit come down on Jesus as he was baptised (see 32,33). This will have reminded John of the way God introduces his servant in the Old Testament: *Here is my servant, whom I uphold, my chosen one in whom I delight; I will put my Spirit on him, and he will bring justice to the nations* (Isa 42:1).

This is what John says: Jesus is God's Lamb (29) and God's Chosen One (34). And we are being invited to make up our own minds as to who Jesus is.

3. – What Andrew says (35-42)

Next day John the Baptist announces once again that Jesus is the Lamb of God, but this time we know who he is talking to (see 35-36). Hearing this prompts the two disciples of John to follow Jesus: this is the one John has been telling them about.

After they have met Jesus and spent some hours talking to him (see 37-39), they are convinced. One of these two disciples is Andrew; we don't know the name of the other one, but it may well have been John the Gospel-writer. But the focus is on Andrew. His priority now is to tell his brother Simon about Jesus: *We have found the Messiah* (41).

When Jesus meets Simon he knows his name and then gives him a new one: Peter (see 42b). We don't learn at this point how Simon reacts to this encounter because the emphasis is on Andrew's verdict as to the identity of Jesus: he is the Messiah, the promised saviour.

Once again John the Gospel-writer is inviting us to make our own decision.

4. – What Nathanael says (43-49)

After Philip has answered Jesus' call to follow him (see 43-44) he tells his friend Nathanael that Jesus of Nazareth is the Messiah (though he doesn't use the word, see 45). But Nathanael is sceptical: *Nazareth! Can anything good come from there?* (46)

Brought to Jesus by Philip, Nathanael is impacted by Jesus knowing all about him (see 47-48). This prompts him to make his own decision: *Rabbi, you are the Son of God; you are the king of Israel* (49).

Nathanael is not saying two things about Jesus here, but one. The phrase *Son of God* was commonly used in the first century to mean *Messiah*, the saviour promised in the Old Testament (see, for example, 2 Sam 7:14). But this was understood almost exclusively to be a political figure who would throw the Romans out of Israel: which is why Nathanael adds that Jesus is *the king of Israel.*

But John is surely thinking that Nathanael is saying more than he knows: Jesus really is the Son of God, in a unique eternal relationship with God the Father (see, for example, chapter 1:14,18 and 5:19-30).

And because of that, it's important to hear what he says about himself.

5. – What Jesus says (50-51)

In his reply to Nathanael Jesus says that he is *the Son of Man* (51b). Sometimes in the Gospels this phrase is simply another way of referring to oneself (compare Matt 16:13 with Mark 8:27 for an example of this).

But in using this expression of himself Jesus is more often referring to the glorious Son of Man seen by the Old Testament prophet Daniel: *In my vision at night I looked, and there before me was one like a son of man, coming with the clouds of heaven. He approached the Ancient of Days and was led into his presence* (Dan 7:13). We will have reason to come back to the title *Son of Man* as we move through the Gospel.

Jesus is also referring here to an incident in the life of Jacob, who *had a dream in which he saw a stairway resting on the earth, with its top reaching to heaven, and the angels of God were ascending and descending on it. There above it stood the Lord...* (Gen 28:12-13a).

For Jacob this was life-changing: *How awesome is this place! This is none other than the house of God; this is the gate of heaven* (Gen 28:17).

Jesus tells his new friends here that they will see the angels of God *ascending and descending on the Son of Man* (51). He is telling them that *he* is now the place where people can meet God.

What Jesus says about himself is the climax to John's introduction to his Gospel. One man has just been impressed by Jesus' knowledge about him; but, says Jesus to Andrew, John, Peter, Philip and Nathanael, *You will see greater things than that* (50). In other words: *You ain't seen nothing yet.*

John's skilful writing is prompting us to do two things. First, to ask ourselves this question about Jesus: *Who is this man?*

And, second, to keep reading his Gospel.

Learning the Gospel

The mirror links in the first half of John's Introduction make the headings easy to learn. And it will not be difficult to learn the headings in the second half.

John's Introduction

A. Jesus: the Word of God

    a. The supremacy of Jesus
    b. John the Baptist and Jesus
    c. Reactions to Jesus
    b'. John the Baptist and Jesus
    a'. The supremacy of Jesus

B. Jesus: who is this man?

    1. What Isaiah says
    2. What John says
    3. What Andrew says
    4. What Nathanael says
    5. What Jesus says

Meeting the Lord

As you run through John's Introduction in your mind you will find that you will remember some of the details of each paragraph. So as you do, please take time to worship Jesus for who he is, and then for what he has come to do.

John wrote his Gospel not only so that we will *believe* in Jesus. He wants us to *meet* him too.

The John experiment is an invitation to do just this.

How to help your memory

1. **Make learning visual** by remembering where the events are on the page of your Bible.
2. **Make learning audible** by learning out loud.
3. **Make learning practical** by doing a little every day.
4. **Make learning enjoyable** by using the experiment to help you pray and worship.

Section One: The Message (John 2:1 - 4:42)

We have already seen in John's Introduction that the Gospel is all about Jesus. Those who encounter him ask themselves the question *Who is this man?* Now Jesus demonstrates that he has come to replace the old with the new: he shows this both in his actions and in his words. That is what this first section is about. It's the message everyone needed to hear *then*, and it's the message everyone needs to hear *now*.

He made a whip out of cords,
and drove all from the temple courts,
both sheep and cattle;
he scattered the coins of the money-changers
and overturned their tables.

John 2:15

Enjoying the View

Two signs

A. The wedding at Cana (2:1-12)

1. Jesus the guest (1-5)
2. Jesus the host (6-10)
3. Reaction: real faith (11-12)

B. Judgment in the temple (2:13-25)

1. Jesus judges the temple (13-17)
2. Jesus replaces the temple (18-22)
3. Reaction: superficial faith (23-25)

Three blocks

X. Jesus and Nicodemus (3:1-21)

1. What the Spirit does (3-10)
2. What the Son says (11-15)
3. What the Father offers (16-21)

Y. The truth about Jesus (3:22-36)

1. What John the Baptist says (22-30)
2. What John the Gospel-writer says (31-36)

Z. Jesus and the Samaritan woman (4:1-42)

1. He's a Jew (7-9)
2. He's greater than Jacob (10-15)
3. He's a prophet (16-24)
4. He's the Messiah (25-42)

John has organised this section – like all the others – around two signs and three blocks. The signs have something in common: they demonstrate that Jesus is replacing the staleness of first-century Jewish religion with something new.

The three blocks underline this message. First, Jesus tells a leading religious teacher about the new birth, which is a mark of the new covenant replacing the old covenant. In the second block John the Baptist's attitude shows the greatness of Jesus, and John the Gospel-writer gives us a summary of the Jesus message so far. And in the third block Jesus reveals his identity to a Samaritan woman and tells her that he will make all temple buildings redundant.

And all three blocks are about the message Jesus came to bring.

Before reading further it would be good to read through John 2:1 - 4:42. As you read you may find yourself talking to Jesus and worshipping him.

Unpacking the Content

Two signs

Sign A. The wedding at Cana (2:1-12)

1. – Jesus the guest (1-5)

Why does Jesus' mother tell him that the wine has run out (see 3)? It looks like she is hoping that he will put this embarrassing situation right.

Jesus replies with *Woman, why do you involve me? (…) My hour has not yet come* (4). By addressing Mary in this way Jesus is not being unfriendly, but he is clearly telling her that it is not for her to set the agenda for his life, but God. Jesus uses the phrase *my hour* a number of times in John's Gospel (see also 7:30; 8:20; 12:23,27; 13:1; 17:1): it refers to Jesus being glorified, a process which will begin with his crucifixion.

The message is clear: Jesus' timetable will not be set by his mother, but by his Father.

2. – Jesus the host (6-10)

Now Jesus is going to turn water into wine. But first John goes to the trouble of telling us where the water is going to come from: *Nearby stood six stone water jars, the kind used by the Jews for ceremonial washing, each holding from eighty to a hundred and twenty litres* (6).

John is saying that this miracle is not just a historical event: it *means* something too.

As the prophets of the Old Testament looked forward to a time when God would make everything new, they often used the image of wine as they proclaimed God's message: *New wine will drip from the mountains and flow from all the hills, and I will bring my people Israel back from exile* (Amos 9:13b-14a).

So as we watch the servants filling the jars with water and taking some to the man running the wedding reception (see 7-8), and as we see his astonishment at the quality of the wine Jesus has created (see 9-10), John is telling us that Jesus is doing much more than helping people out of an embarrassing situation.

Jesus is *acting out* his message: he is replacing the water used for ceremonial washing (which stands for old religion) with the best wine (which stands for the new life he has come to bring).

3. – Reaction: real faith (11-12)

It is no wonder that what Jesus does here is *the first of the signs through which he revealed his glory* (11). John has already told us that this is *the glory of the one and only Son, who came from the Father* (see chapter 1:14). What we have seen Jesus do at the wedding at Cana, only God can do.

And, says John, *his disciples believed in him* (11b). Of course we don't know how much they've understood, but their faith is growing and it's *real*.

In Mark's Gospel Jesus is recorded as announcing that he is bringing new wine. In a passage where he uses wedding language (see Mark 2:19), Jesus says: *And no one pours new wine into old wineskins. Otherwise, the wine will burst the skins, and both the wine and the wineskins will be ruined. No, they pour new wine into new wineskins* (Mark 2:22).

It's the same message. Jesus is the new wine; the old wineskins are the religious leaders; and the new wineskins are the people who decide to believe in Jesus and follow him.

Here in chapter 2 of his Gospel John is inviting us, his readers, to trust in Jesus, too (see also chapter 1:12-13; 20:30-31).

Sign B. Judgment in the temple (2:13-25)

This passage presents us with a puzzle. John tells us about this incident at the *beginning* of Jesus' public ministry, while Matthew, Mark and Luke record it towards the *end*. Who's right?

Let me tell you my own view. I think there is good evidence that John is very concerned to tell the Jesus story in the right order, so my guess is that this incident in the temple really did happen near the start. As to whether the other Gospel-writers record this near the end because they choose to record Jesus visiting Jerusalem only once, or because Jesus in fact cleared the temple on two occasions: well, you pays your money and you takes your choice.

(For more on this, see Appendix 1, Question 1. But there is much more in the larger commentaries.)

1. – Jesus judges the temple (13-17)

There were three Jewish festivals for which most adult males in Israel were expected to go to Jerusalem (see Deut 16:16), and Passover is one of them (see 13). So Jesus is there with his disciples, who are watching and listening.

Jesus walks into the temple as if he owns the place, which he does (see 14-16). But instead of seeing the glory of God, which points to God's reality and presence (see 1 Kings 8:10-11), he is confronted with something that fills him with anger (see 14-15): *To those who sold doves he said 'Get these out of here! Stop turning my Father's house into a market!'* (16)

This is judgment because there is no glory here. And John tells us that the disciples *remembered that it is written: 'Zeal for your house will consume me'* (17, Ps 69:9).

John wants us to see that Jesus is rejecting the sorry state of old religion and putting something new in its place. What is that new thing? That is about to become clear.

2. – Jesus replaces the temple (18-22)

The Jewish leaders (which is normally what John means when he uses the expression *the Jews*) demand a sign to prove that Jesus has the right to clear the temple like this (see 18).

Jesus' reply *Destroy this temple, and I will raise it again in three days* (19) causes confusion, because they think Jesus is talking about the temple building.

But now he is using the word *temple* in another sense. John spells it out for us: *But the temple he had spoken of was his body* (21).

The disciples only understood this later (see 22), but John wants us to understand it now. In judging the temple Jesus is declaring that it is redundant, and that *he* is the new temple.

It should have been possible to see the glory of God in the temple building, but it wasn't there. And John has already told us where we can see the glory of God: in Jesus himself (see chapter 1:14; 2:11).

Jesus replaces the temple: this is a key part of his message.

3. – Reaction: superficial faith (23-25)

Many people, says John, *believed* (23). But Jesus is not moved by this (see 24), probably because their faith was based only on his signs (see 23).

There is a contrast between the disciples' real faith (see 11) and many other people's superficial faith. John makes it clear: *But Jesus would not entrust himself to them, for he knew all people. He did not need any testimony about mankind, for he knew what was in each person* (24-25).

The two signs at the beginning of Section One are very different from one another, but the message is the same: Jesus has come to replace the staleness of dead religion with the new life of his presence and glory. If we want to see the glory of God we need to look at Jesus.

And if we recognise him it makes sense to believe in him.

Three blocks

As we read these three blocks we will see that each of them, in its own way, underlines the message which Jesus has already been communicating in his signs.

Block X. Jesus and Nicodemus (3:1-21)

Now a man who is a leading figure in first-century Judaism comes to see Jesus (see 1). Some people think he comes *at night* (2) because he wants this visit to be secret; I am more inclined to think that Nicodemus is looking for an uninterrupted conversation.

And for a very good reason. John has only described one of Jesus' signs in Jerusalem (see chapter 2:13-17), but Nicodemus has heard about others (2; see also chapter 2:23), and perhaps even seen them for himself. For him the conclusion is obvious: Jesus is *from God* (2). But he is not yet entirely convinced.

1. – What the Spirit does (3-10)

Nicodemus may well be wanting Jesus to talk about the kingdom of God. He will not be disappointed, but he *will* be puzzled: *Very truly I tell you, no one can see the kingdom of God unless they are born again* (3). Nicodemus' reply in verse 4 shows that he has no idea what Jesus is talking about.

Born again is certainly the right translation here, though the phrase can also mean *born from above*, which will remind us of chapter 1:12-13.

People who receive Jesus by believing in him, are able to do that because God has given them new birth from heaven. The new birth is something the Spirit does.

But what *is* the new birth? Jesus starts to explain: *Very truly I tell you, no one can enter the kingdom of God unless they are born of water and the Spirit* (5). However, even after listening to Jesus unpack this, Nicodemus still doesn't understand: *How can this be?* (9)

What comes now is going to tell us where we will find the explanation of *born of water and the Spirit: 'You are Israel's teacher,' said Jesus, 'and do you not understand these things?'* (10) In other words Jesus is saying *Nicodemus, this should all sound familiar: it's in the Old Testament!*

There are three main passages in the Old Testament which promise that God will one day replace the old covenant with the new covenant, in which everyone who trusts him will know God deeply and be completely forgiven. Have a look at what God promises:

> *I will sprinkle clean water on you, and you will be clean;*
> *I will cleanse you from all your impurities and from all your idols.*
> *I will give you a new heart and put a new spirit in you;*
> *I will remove from you your heart of stone and give you a heart of flesh.*
> *And I will put my Spirit in you and move you to follow my decrees and be careful to keep my laws.*
> (Ezek 36:25-27; see also Jer 31:31-34 and Joel 2:28-32)

Water and Spirit. Doesn't this sound like a new birth?

And the message is clear: this new birth which brings us into the kingdom of God, where we experience God's forgiveness and power, is something the Spirit does in us.

2. – What the Son says (11-15)

Now Jesus uses another passage from the Old Testament to help Nicodemus understand how this new covenant relationship with God is possible. And he refers to himself again here as the Son of Man (see 13-14, and my comments on chapter 1:51).

But let's look at the Old Testament background first.

The people of Israel in the wilderness had been grumbling against God, so God punished them by sending snakes: all those who were bitten, died (see Numbers 21:4-9 for the full story). In response to Moses' prayer God said to him *Make a snake and put it up on a pole; anyone who is bitten can look at it and live* (Num 21:8).

So that's what Moses did: *Then when anyone was bitten by a snake and looked at the bronze snake, they lived* (Num 21:9b).

Now let's read what the Son says: *Just as Moses lifted up the snake in the wilderness, so the Son of Man must be lifted up* (14). Jesus is going to be *lifted up*: after the nails have been driven through his hands, he will be lifted up as the cross is raised and then dropped into the ground.

There is a play on words here. *Lifted up* doesn't only mean *raised up*, it also means *exalted*. Jesus hasn't yet spelt out how he will die, but for us who are in the know, the message is clear: if we want to see Jesus exalted, we should look at the cross.

And this has a wonderful result. Jesus tells Nicodemus (and us) that *the Son of Man must be lifted up, that everyone who believes may have eternal life in him* (14b-15).

This is why Jesus came, and it's why John is writing his Gospel (see chapter 20:30-31).

3. – What the Father offers (16-21)

Opinions differ as to whether Jesus is still speaking in this paragraph (there are no inverted commas in Greek). To me it reads more like John's commentary on what Nicodemus has learnt from Jesus. But in any case we get a summary here of what God the Father offers.

For God so loved the world that he gave his one and only Son, that whoever believes in him shall not perish but have eternal life (16). John has already used the expression *one and only Son* in his Introduction (see chapter 1:14,18); now he tells us that the Father *gave* him because he *loved* us. And the promise of *life* for all who *believe* is repeated too.

John wants us to take time to look at what the Father offers.

God sent his Son, says John, *to save the world through him* (17) and he underlines how important our response is to Jesus: *Whoever believes in him is not condemned but whoever does not believe stands condemned already because they have not believed in the name of God's one and only Son* (18).

So there are two responses, both of which have eternal consequences.

The negative response (see 19-20) involves a refusal to own up about the wrong things in our hearts; *the positive response* (see 21) means no longer hiding but living openly in God's presence.

Being accepted by God and a new quality of life that goes on for ever: this is what the Father offers through his Son Jesus.

John tells us about the encounter between Jesus and Nicodemus by referring to all three members of the Trinity. The Father did something in eternity past: he loved us and decided to send Jesus to rescue us. The Son did something 2,000 years ago: he agreed to be lifted up on the cross so we could experience real life. And the Spirit is doing something today: he is giving people new birth so that they can see who Jesus is and why he came.

This is all part of the message of Jesus. If it makes us want to thank God the Father and worship him for his astonishing love in sending Jesus, that is another piece of evidence that the Spirit has done the miracle of new birth in our hearts.

Block Y. The truth about Jesus (3:22-36)

1. – What John the Baptist says (22-30)

John is still baptising (see 23), but now Jesus' disciples are baptising people, too (see 22 and chapter 4:2). When John hears that more people are going to Jesus than coming to him (see 26), he is delighted because he knows who Jesus is.

First, he says that Jesus is the Messiah: *I am not the Messiah but am sent ahead of him* (28). John has been clear about this from the outset (see chapter 1:23,33).

And second, John says that Jesus is the bridegroom: *The friend who attends the bridegroom waits and listens for him, and is full of joy when he hears the bridegroom's voice* (29). It seems like you can't talk about Jesus and his message without using wedding language (see chapter 2:1-10 and Mark 2:19-20). The best man wants the bridegroom to be the centre of attention: he doesn't want to steal the show.

But now John has heard the voice of Jesus the bridegroom. He says: *That joy is mine; and it is now complete* (29b).

And so John the signpost says this about his relationship with Jesus: *He must become greater; I must become less* (30). This is the last time we hear John speaking in this Gospel. With these words John the Baptist sums up the purpose of everything he has done: it's like he's saying *Don't look at me; look at Jesus!*

2. – What John the Gospel-writer says (31-36)

There are differing views as to whether John the Baptist is still speaking here. But I think it much more likely that John the Gospel-writer is now commenting on the story so far and giving his readers a summary of the Jesus message.

John tells us the difference between Jesus and John the Baptist: *The one who comes from above is above all; the one who is from the earth belongs to the earth* (31a). And Jesus *speaks the words of God* (34). There is a reason for this: God has given the Spirit *without limit* to Jesus (34b).

That phrase should make us catch our breath. The Bible never says this about anyone else: only with Jesus does God never stop pouring his Spirit into him. And so John tells us the truth about Jesus: *The Father loves the Son and has placed everything in his hands* (35).

This may be a good moment to stop reading and to worship Jesus.

We have already seen how John stresses that human response to Jesus is crucial (see chapter 1:9-13 and 20:30-31). Now he ends Block Y of Section One of his Gospel by expressing the options as clearly as he knows how: *Whoever believes in the Son has eternal life, but whoever rejects the Son will not see life, for God's wrath remains on them* (36).

John is calling on us, his readers, to decide what our response to Jesus will be.

Block Z. Jesus and the Samaritan woman (4:1-42)

This last part of Section One takes us, once again, to the heart of the Jesus message. First-century Judaism was centred on the temple in Jerusalem and was convinced, for the most part, that the God of Israel was not interested in people from other nations.

Just as Jesus overturned the tables in the temple (see chapter 2:13-17), he now overturns some of the assumptions of first-century Judaism. He speaks to a Samaritan. In some ways the Samaritans were viewed even more negatively than Gentiles: they were ethnically impure because of intermarriage with other nations and had built their own temple on Mount Gerizim. A Jew who wanted to insult a fellow-Jew might even call them a Samaritan (see chapter 8:48).

To get from Jerusalem back up to Galilee, John tells us that Jesus *had to go through Samaria* (4). Although there were other available routes, most Jews would choose to go through Samaria because it reduced journey time. So it may well be that Jesus *had to* go through Samaria because he knew that his Father had made an appointment for him in Sychar (see 5).

John tells us that Jesus, *tired as he was from the journey, sat down by the well* (6). The stage is set for a conversation in which a Samaritan woman will make her own journey as she changes her mind as to who Jesus is. The progression through the passage is clear.

1. – He's a Jew (7-9)

The Samaritan woman has come to draw water. When Jesus asks her for a drink she is astonished: *You are a Jew, and I am a Samaritan woman. How can you ask me for a drink?* (9a) John explains her surprise by telling us that *Jews do not associate with Samaritans* (9b).

The woman will have recognised that Jesus is a Jew by the clothes he was wearing. This is all she knows about him, but her journey has begun.

2. – He's greater than Jacob (10-15)

At this point the woman is sceptical: *Are you greater than our father Jacob..?* (12a) What prompts her question is Jesus' words *If you knew the gift of God and who it is that asks you for a drink, you would have asked him and he would have given you living water* (10), as well as the fact that she is drawing water from Jacob's well (see 5-6).

In the Old Testament God describes himself as the spring of living water (Jer 2:13 and 17:13) and links the image of water with the gift of his Spirit: *I will pour water on the thirsty land, and streams on the dry ground; I will pour out my Spirit on your offspring, and my blessing on your descendants* (Isa 44:3).

The woman will not have picked up the allusion: the Samaritan Bible consisted only of the first five books of what we call the Old Testament.

If Jesus was thirsty at the beginning of this encounter, now the woman is thirsty: *Sir, give me this water so that I won't get thirsty and have to keep coming here to draw water* (15).

But there is more to come.

3. – He's a prophet (16-24)

When Jesus asks her to get her husband, the woman admits that she doesn't have one (see 16-17a). Now comes the shock. Jesus says to her: *You are right when you say you have no husband. The fact is, you have had five husbands, and the man you now have is not your husband. What you have just said is quite true* (17b-18).

For the woman there is only one possible conclusion: Jesus is a prophet (see 19). So, because he obviously has access to divine knowledge, she asks about the biggest issue which divided Jews and Samaritans: *Our ancestors worshipped on this mountain, but you Jews claim that the place where we must worship is in Jerusalem* (20). It's like she's saying *Who's right?*

This takes us to the heart of Jesus' message. Questions about temples miss the point, because Jesus is replacing the water of old religion with the wine of his own presence. He tells the woman that *a time is coming when you will worship the Father neither on this mountain nor in Jerusalem* (21).

So this Jew is not claiming special status for their temple down south; instead he is saying that *a time is coming and has now come when the true worshippers will worship the Father in the Spirit and in truth, for they are the kind of worshippers the Father seeks* (23).

This is extraordinary stuff. The woman knows that Jesus is a prophet, and here he is, *not* excluding Samaritans but saying that *God is Spirit and his worshippers must worship in the Spirit and in truth* (24).

4. – He's the Messiah (25-42)

In calling Jesus a prophet the Samaritan woman may have had the promise to Moses of the Prophet-Messiah in mind (see Deut 18:18). In any case she says that she knows that the Messiah will come one day (see 25).

Jesus now makes the claim that this whole conversation has been leading up to: *I, the one speaking to you – I am he* (26b).

The woman is convinced. She runs back to town and tells everyone *Come, see a man who told me everything I've ever done. Could this be the Messiah?* (29) My guess is that the townspeople see at once that something has transformed her, which is why they want to meet this man for themselves (see 30).

But while they are on their way, Jesus' disciples are back from their shopping trip (see 8) and encouraging him to eat something (see 31). But it is fulfilling his Father's plan that gives Jesus energy: *My food... is to do the will of him who sent me and to finish his work* (34). We should remember that Jesus knows that finishing his Father's work will involve the cross.

Back at the wedding in Cana we noted that Amos 9:13-14 provides a background to Jesus turning water into wine (see chapter 2:6-10). Now he refers to the same passage as he tells his disciples that everywhere there is a harvest of people longing for the Messiah (see 35-38).

Even in Samaria!

John returns to the theme of people responding to Jesus (see chapter 1:9-14 and chapter 20:30-31). Many in Sychar believe in Jesus (see 39), but that is just the beginning. Jesus stays with them for two days *and because of his words many more became believers* (41).

The message of Jesus could be summed up like this: *Out with the old; in with the new.* Jesus has come to replace the water of religion, its rituals and temple, with the wine of his glory and presence. And this is not just for Israel: it's for everyone.

So Section One reaches a wonderful climax as John tells us what the Samaritans say to the woman about Jesus: *We no longer believe just because of what you said; now we have heard for ourselves, and we know that this man really is the Saviour of the world* (42).

Learning the Gospel

The structure of Section One makes it easy to learn. First, just learn the headings in bold: and remember that there are two signs, followed by three blocks.

Now learn the sub-headings for the first sign: The wedding at Cana. Just getting these headings in your mind will remind you of what happens in the passage.

Then work on the sub-headings for the second sign: Judgment in the temple. Once again this will help you to start remembering details from the incident.

Now go through the same process with each of the three blocks.

You may find this easier to do if you have arranged with a friend to meet up after you have both learnt the order of the events in Section One.

Learning Section One can be done in about ten minutes. And it's worth it.

Section One: The Message

Two signs

A. The wedding at Cana

1. Jesus the guest
2. Jesus the host
3. Reaction: real faith

B. Judgment in the temple

1. Jesus judges the temple
2. Jesus replaces the temple
3. Reaction: superficial faith

Three blocks

X. Jesus and Nicodemus

1. What the Spirit does
2. What the Son says
3. What the Father offers

Y. The truth about Jesus

1. What John the Baptist says
2. What John the Gospel-writer says

Z. Jesus and the Samaritan woman

1. He's a Jew
2. He's greater than Jacob
3. He's a prophet
4. He's the Messiah

Meeting the Lord

Once you have committed the structure to memory, start to tell the events of the section to yourself, or to a friend, including as many details as you remember. As you do this, the Holy Spirit will be using the Jesus story in your life.

You will notice that the message of *Out with the old, in with the new* comes several times. Thank Jesus that he came to replace the old religion with the new life of his presence; thank him for his love in being willing to be lifted up on the cross to earn your forgiveness; thank him for giving you new birth by his Holy Spirit; and thank him for coming to be the Saviour of *the world.*

This is the John experiment: as you re-tell John you will rediscover Jesus.

Section Two: The Authority (John 4:43 - 5:47)

In Section One we saw and heard the Jesus message: he has come to offer something new to all those who trust him. Now in Section Two we encounter Jesus' authority: first in two healings, and then as he explains his unique relationship with God the Father. And, all the while, the opposition from the religious leaders is growing. This is a reminder for John's readers that everyone needs to make their mind up as to how they will respond to Jesus.

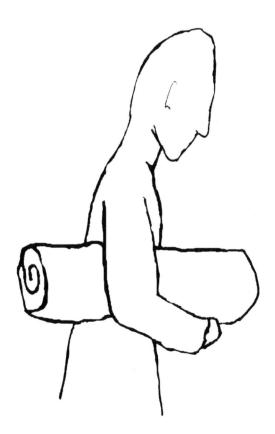

Then Jesus said to him,
'Get up! Pick up your mat and walk.'
At once the man was cured; he picked up his mat and walked.
The day on which this took place was a Sabbath.

John 5:8-9

Enjoying the View

Two signs

A. Jesus heals a royal official's son (4:43-54)

1. Great need (46-47)
2. Effortless authority (48-50a)
3. Growing faith (50b-54)

B. Jesus heals a paralysed man (5:1-15)

1. Great need (1-3)
2. Effortless authority (5-9a)
3. Growing opposition (9b-15)

Three blocks

X. The claim (5:16-30)

a. Jesus and the Father (19-20a)
b. Jesus the life-giver (20b-21)
c. Jesus the judge (22-23)
d. Jesus and us (24)
c'. Jesus the judge (25-27)
b'. Jesus the life-giver (28-29)
a'. Jesus and the Father (30)

Y. The evidence (5:31-40)

1. What John says (31-35)
2. What Jesus does (36)
3. What Scripture says (37-40)

Z. The diagnosis (5:41-47)

1. They don't love God (41-44)
2. They don't believe Moses (45-47)

Once again, John has structured this section around two signs and three blocks, making it easy to commit to memory.

The signs have two things in common: they show Jesus in total control as he exercises his authority, and each results in a response to Jesus, positive after the first and negative after the second. This is a pattern we have already seen after the two signs back in Section One (see chapter 2).

The blocks are an opportunity to hear Jesus teaching at length for the first time in this Gospel. First he makes claims as to his identity; second he provides the evidence to help us believe him; and third he explains why the reaction of the religious leaders is so negative.

This time there is a contrast with the previous section, which ended with an overwhelmingly positive response to Jesus from people in Samaria (see chapter 4:39-42). At the end of Section Two, however, we see exactly the opposite from the religious leaders in Jerusalem.

It would be good to read through John 4:43 - 5:47 before going on. Be ready to meet Jesus: it is only a short step from reading to worship.

Unpacking the Content

Two signs

Sign A. Jesus heals a royal official's son (4:43-54)

The opening few verses here present us with a puzzle. Jesus knew that *a prophet has no honour in his own country* (44), but *when he arrived in Galilee, the Galileans welcomed him* (45a). What's going on here?

John may have given us a clue: *They had seen all that he had done in Jerusalem at the Passover Festival, for they also had been there* (45b). It looks like this is another example of a positive response to Jesus being based solely on signs (see chapter 2:23-25). Jesus will say something similar here in verse 48.

1. – Great need (46-47)

The royal official who comes to Jesus is probably a Jew, though we can't be sure. What we do know is that his son is not only ill, but seriously ill: he is *close to death* (47). So this is a situation of great need: we can imagine the man's desperation as he rides to Cana and begs Jesus for help.

2. – Effortless authority (48-50a)

The official is not put off by Jesus' complaint that many people will only believe if they see him performing signs (see 48), because he repeats his request: *Sir, come down before my child dies* (49).

The response is immediate: *'Go,' Jesus replied, 'your son will live'* (50a). So great is his authority that Jesus can just say the word; what's more, he clearly knows that he can heal the boy from a distance.

This is effortless authority.

3. – Growing faith (50b-54)

Somehow the boy's father is sure of Jesus' authority, too: *the man took Jesus at his word and departed* (50b). John's choice of words here seems to stress the fact that the official is not acting on the basis of signs he has seen or heard about, but simply trusting what Jesus has said. This is faith in action.

On his way home the royal official meets some of his servants coming to tell him that his son has recovered; they tell him, too, what time the miracle had happened (see 52). John adds: *Then the father realised that this was the exact time at which Jesus had said to him, 'Your son will live'* (53a).

Now we learn about a second miracle: *So he and his whole household believed* (53b).

This Gospel, and every incident in it, has been written to encourage us to believe in Jesus (see chapter 20:30-31). Here, John wants us to see faith growing in this man, and to see it spreading to his family and his servants.

This was the second sign Jesus performed after coming from Judea to Galilee (54). We know that there had been other signs – in Jerusalem (see chapter 2:23; 3:1-2; 4:45). But this is the second sign Jesus performed in the region where he had grown up.

Signs should not be the reason people believe in Jesus, but they may point us in the right direction. Here they are a signpost showing us Jesus' authority.

Sign B. Jesus heals a paralysed man (5:1-15)

For this second sign in Section Two, Jesus is in Jerusalem again (see 1), just as he had been for the second sign in Section One (see chapter 2:13).

1. – Great need (1-3)

John is careful to tell us where we are: *Now there is in Jerusalem near the Sheep Gate a pool, which in Aramaic is called Bethesda and which is surrounded by five covered colonnades* (2).

There is suffering everywhere you look: *Here a great number of disabled people used to lie – the blind, the lame, the paralysed* (3).

2. – Effortless authority (5-9a)

Jesus focuses on a man who has been unable to walk for 38 years (see 5).

He asks him *Do you want to get well?* (6b) The question is probably aimed at finding out if the man has faith, or if he is simply resigned to his fate.

The paralysed man doesn't answer the question directly, though his complaint that he has no one to help him into the pool *when the water is stirred* (7) suggests that the answer is *Yes*.

In any case Jesus is going to show his authority. He doesn't need the water in the pool; instead, he simply gives the command *Get up! Pick up your mat and walk* (8b). And John tells us that *at once the man was cured; he picked up his mat and walked* (9a).

This is an authority as great as Jesus demonstrated in the healing of the royal official's son.

3. – Growing opposition (9b-15)

John tells us that *the day on which this took place was a Sabbath* (9b). By healing this man on the Sabbath day Jesus is claiming authority on a level which can only be described as daring.

So the religious leaders need to discover the identity of the healer, not because he has healed but because he has healed *on the Sabbath* (see 9b-12).

The Sabbath law had become one of the most important in first-century Israel, and for good reason. Loving God with all your heart, soul, mind and strength was central, but only God could know if you were doing it. But if there were enough people watching, they could find out if you were keeping all the Sabbath rules.

At first the religious leaders have difficulty unearthing the name of the Sabbath-breaking healer: *the man who was healed had no idea who it was, for Jesus had slipped away into the crowd* (13).

John tells us that Jesus looked for the man in the temple and said to him *See, you are well again. Stop sinning, or something worse may happen to you* (14). And now, far from showing any desire to protect Jesus from the authorities' opposition, *the man went away and told the Jewish leaders that it was Jesus who had made him well* (15).

It's like this man, healed by Jesus, has joined the opposition. The stage is set for the confrontation to come.

Three blocks

Block X. The claim (5:16-30)

There are two reasons why the religious leaders see Jesus as their enemy. The first is that he *was doing these things on the Sabbath* (16), and the second is what Jesus says in his defence: *My Father is always at his work to this very day, and I too am working* (17).

This is their objection: by calling God his Father Jesus is *making himself equal with God* (18b).

This needs some unpacking. Everyone in the first century agreed that God worked on the Sabbath, but that didn't mean he was breaking it: he was God after all. Now Jesus is saying that it is OK for him to heal on the Sabbath because he comes into the same category as God. In other words it is like he is claiming to be a second God.

You can feel the tension. Is Jesus going to back down? How is he going to explain himself?

In verses 19-30 Jesus makes extraordinary claims; the passage is structured around mirror links to make the argument clearer and learning it easier.

a. – Jesus and the Father (19-20a)

Jesus now makes it clear that he is not thinking of himself as a second God: *The Son can do nothing by himself; he can only do what he sees his Father doing, because whatever the Father does the Son also does* (19).

So Jesus never acts independently of the Father, and it is the Father who grasps the initiative: Jesus submits to him.

And there's nothing cold and distant about this, says Jesus, for *the Father loves the Son and shows him all he does* (20a).

b. – Jesus the life-giver (20b-21)

In the first century it was common to stress two divine characteristics especially: only God gives life, and only God is the judge. Now Jesus' claims become even more amazing (see 20b): *For just as the Father raises the dead and gives them life, even so the Son gives life to whom he is pleased to give it* (21).

Jesus is claiming to be able to give people physical and spiritual life, just as God the Father can do those things. No one else would dare claim such a thing: Jesus is doing the opposite of backing down.

c. – Jesus the judge (22-23)

Moreover, says Jesus, *the Father judges no one, but has entrusted all judgment to the Son* (22). This could not be any clearer: the judge on Judgment Day will be Jesus.

So Jesus is not only claiming to be the life-giver. He is claiming to be the judge, too.

But there is something even more shocking to come. *Why* has the Father entrusted all judgment to Jesus? Because he desires *that all may honour the Son just as they honour the Father* (23a).

Some people are happy to honour God but ignore Jesus. But Jesus says that won't do: *Whoever does not honour the Son does not honour the Father, who sent him* (23b). If you turn your back on Jesus the Son you are turning your back on God the Father, too.

d. – Jesus and us (24)

This verse stands at the centre of the mirror linking and is an invitation for everyone willing to accept it: *Very truly I tell you, whoever hears my word and believes him who sent me has eternal life and will not be judged but has crossed over from death to life* (24).

This is good news. The person who hears Jesus and trusts the Father *has* (not *will* have) eternal life; they *have* crossed over (not *will* cross over) from death to life.

It's a done deal. Because of Jesus.

c'. – Jesus the judge (25-27)

Jesus describes himself here in two ways.

First, he's *the Son of God* (25), in a unique relationship with God the Father. John makes this very clear in his Gospel (see chapter 1:14,18; 20:31).

And second, he's *the Son of Man* (27), the one described by Daniel the prophet (see Dan 7:13-14 and my comments on chapter 1:51).

And here is the claim again: Jesus says that God the Father has *given him authority to judge* (27, see also part c).

b'. – Jesus the life-giver (28-29)

Jesus tells his hearers not to be amazed (see 28, and also 20b in the mirror link b/b'). On the last day, when Jesus says the word, *all who are in their graves will hear his voice and come out* (28b-29a): he will give them life so they can appear before him for judgment (see 29).

a'. – Jesus and the Father (30)

Once again Jesus makes clear that he never acts independently of his Father, but submits to him: *By myself I can do nothing; (...) I seek not to please myself but him who sent me* (30, and see also 19a in the mirror link a/a').

In verses 19-30 we have heard the claim of Jesus: he is in a unique relationship with the Father, he is the life-giver and the judge of all. Verse 24 ties it all together: if we *believe,* the life-giver will give us *eternal life* and we *will not be condemned* by the judge.

John is surely wanting us to make up our own minds as to how we will respond to the claims of Jesus.

Block Y. The evidence (5:31-40)

In his signs and in his teaching Jesus has been demonstrating authority. But is he telling the truth? Here, following the Old Testament (see Deut 19:15b) he gives his listeners three reasons why we should believe his claims.

1. – What John says (31-35)

The emphasis in this paragraph is on John the Baptist: *John was a lamp that burned and gave light, and you chose for a time to enjoy his light* (35). The implication is that the religious leaders at some point chose to reject John and the light he brought.

But what John said about Jesus (see chapter 1:19-28) was reliable: *You have sent to John and he has testified to the truth* (33). And, says Jesus, he is reminding the religious leaders about John's words *that you may be saved* (34b).

2. – What Jesus does (36)

Now Jesus points to even stronger evidence: *The works that the Father has given me to finish – the very works that I am doing – testify that the Father has sent me* (36b).

It was this that had convinced Nicodemus that Jesus was the real thing: *No one could perform the signs you are doing if God were not with him* (chapter 3:2b).

3. – What Scripture says (37-40)

Now Jesus returns to what God the Father says about him: he has already spoken in the Scriptures.

Jesus has some praise for the religious leaders: *You study the Scriptures diligently because you think that in them you have eternal life* (39a). But immediately he points to their mistake: *These are the very Scriptures that testify about me, yet you refuse to come to me to have life* (39b-40).

This is a devastating critique. Their rejection of Jesus (see 18a) is not the result of ignorance: they know their Bibles and have read what God has said about his Son, but *you do not believe the one he sent* (38b).

Block Z. The diagnosis (5:41-47)

Jesus now explains *why* the religious leaders are rejecting him and his authority.

1. – They don't love God (41-44)

Jesus confidently says *I know that you do not have the love of God in your hearts* (42b). Imagine how they feel: Jesus is accusing them of breaking the most important commandment (see Deut 6:4-5).

What *is* in the hearts of the religious leaders is a hunger for glory – not glory from God but glory and approval from each other. And this, says Jesus, is what makes it impossible for them to accept him: *How can you believe since you accept glory from one another but do not seek the glory that comes from the only God?* (44)

Instead of *seeking* glory from others they should have been *seeing* the glory of God *in Jesus* (see chapter 1:14,18; 2:11).

But the diagnosis goes further.

2. – They don't believe Moses (45-47)

This will have hurt these leaders almost as much as the first accusation. Moses was their great hero: God had given him the law to hand on to his people.

But Jesus says *Your accuser is Moses, on whom your hopes are set* (45b). He goes on: *If you believed Moses, you would believe me, for he wrote about me* (46, and see chapter 1:45 and Deut 18:15).

Jesus is not mincing his words. John has already told us that Jesus *knew what was in each person* (see chapter 2:25b), and here in this encounter with some of Israel's religious leadership we see the proof of it.

Section Two ends with Jesus asking his opponents a question about their attitude to Moses: *But since you do not believe what he wrote, how are you going to believe what I say?* (47)

Learning the Gospel

Once again, start by learning the headings in bold.

Next, learn the sub-headings for the two signs: you will already find that the details of the incidents will be coming back to you.

Now move on to learn the sub-headings of the three blocks. Part X (The Claim) looks long, but the mirror linking makes it easy to learn.

Remember that it might help to agree with a friend that you will both learn the order of the events in Section Two.

As more and more of the content of the section gets into your memory, it will *change* you. There is power in the word of God!

Section Two: The Authority

Two signs

A. Jesus heals a royal official's son
1. Great need
2. Effortless authority
3. Growing faith

B. Jesus heals a paralysed man
1. Great need
2. Effortless authority
3. Growing opposition

Three blocks

X. The claim
a. Jesus and the Father
b. Jesus the life-giver
c. Jesus the judge

    d. Jesus and us
    c'. Jesus the judge
    b'. Jesus the life-giver
    a'. Jesus and the Father

Y. The evidence
    1. What John says
    2. What Jesus does
    3. What Scripture says

Z. The diagnosis
    1. They don't love God
    2. They don't believe Moses

Meeting the Lord

As you move through the ingredients of Section Two in your mind, tell yourself the story (with as many details as you can remember), or do this with a friend. Then respond to what you have been thinking about by talking to Jesus.

You will be reminded of his authority in the two healings at the start of the section; when thinking about the royal official's growing faith you may want to pray for someone you know who is still at the beginning of that journey; when you consider all that Jesus is claiming about himself in Block X you may well find yourself worshipping him.

One of the main reasons God has given us John's Gospel is so that we can encounter Jesus. He is waiting to meet you.

Section Three: The Training (John 6:1 - 8:59)

The battle lines have been drawn. In Section Two we saw that the religious leaders are implacably opposed to Jesus: they have decided to kill him (see chapter 5:18). Now, in Section Three, Jesus is training his team, teaching the disciples who he is as he interacts with the crowds and as the opposition increases. We will be watching Jesus and listening to him: he wants to train us up too, so that we can tell others the good news.

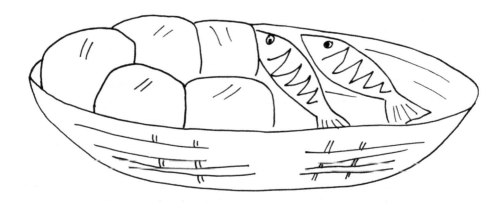

Another of his disciples, Andrew,
Simon Peter's brother, spoke up,
'Here is a boy with five small barley loaves
and two small fish,
but how far will they go among so many?'

John 6:8-9

Enjoying the View

Two signs

A. Jesus feeds the 5,000 (6:1-15)

1. The situation (1-4)
2. The miracle (5-13)
3. The reaction (14-15)

B. Jesus walks on Lake Galilee (6:16-24)

1. The situation (16-18)
2. The miracle (19-21)
3. The reaction (22-24)

Three blocks

X. Jesus: the bread of life (6:25-71)

1. His diagnosis (25-34)
2. His claim (35-48)
3. His explanation (49-59)
4. His question (60-71)

Y. Jesus: the source of water (7:1-52)

1. Jesus' authority (10-24)
2. Jesus' identity (25-36)
3. Jesus' promise (37-44)

Z. Jesus: the light of the world (8:12-59)

1. Jesus' authority (12-30)
2. What Jesus thinks of the crowd (31-47)
3. What the crowd think of Jesus (48-59)

The two signs at the beginning of Section Three show us Jesus training his disciples to recognise who he is. And, after each miracle, as after the signs in Sections One and Two, John tells us how people were reacting.

In the three blocks Jesus is responding to the questions and accusations of the crowd and of some of the religious leaders. And all the time the disciples are learning more about the identity of the man they are following.

Before continuing to read *this* book, it would be good to spend time reading through chapters 6, 7 and 8 in John's. See what strikes you; watch the opposition grow; listen to Jesus.

And use the opportunity to worship and pray.

Unpacking the Content

Two signs

Sign A. Jesus feeds the 5,000 (6:1-15)

This is the only Jesus miracle which is in all four of the Gospels, and in addition Matthew and Mark tell us about the feeding of the 4,000. What is so special about the feeding of a huge crowd?

The answer may be in the prophecy of Isaiah in the Old Testament. In a poetic description of what we might call heaven, Isaiah writes: *On this mountain the Lord Almighty will prepare a feast of rich food for all peoples, a banquet of aged wine – the best of meats and the finest of wines. On this mountain he will destroy the shroud that enfolds all peoples, the sheet that covers all nations; he will swallow up death for ever. The Sovereign Lord will wipe away the tears from all faces; he will remove his people's disgrace from all the earth. The Lord has spoken* (Isa 25:6-8).

In the first century Jews referred to this celebration as *the messianic banquet*: they believed that the host at this feast at the end of time would be the Messiah. And now here is Jesus inviting 5,000 people to a meal.

Could this be a preview of the messianic banquet? If it is, that would make Jesus the Messiah.

1. – The situation (1-4)

John says that many of those following Jesus were fascinated by his signs (2; see also chapter 2:23 and 4:45,48). They don't yet seem to be trusting him, but they are intrigued.

Soon John will tell us that *about five thousand men were there* (10b). Because of this some commentators estimate that, with women and children added into the equation, this might have been a crowd of some 20,000 people.

If it had been, I think John would have told us.

We will understand the situation better if we look at verse 4: *The Jewish Passover Festival was near.* This means that almost every adult male was on his way to Jerusalem (see my comments on chapter 2:13-17). So it makes sense to say that this crowd consisted almost exclusively of around 5,000 men.

2. – The miracle (5-13)

Jesus uses this opportunity to train his disciples. He asks Philip how they are going to provide food for the crowds (see 5), and John explains *he asked this only to test him, for he already had in mind what he was going to do* (6).

Philip is out of his depth, as is Andrew (see 7-9): this is an impossible situation. So now Jesus is ready to perform the sign which will point to his identity.

After thanking his Father for the food, Jesus *distributed to those who were seated as much as they wanted* (11). With those last few words John is making clear that this is a *generous* miracle: from five loaves and two fish (see 9) Jesus is providing more than enough food for a huge crowd. Once again we are seeing his effortless authority.

When the disciples obey Jesus' command to collect the leftovers (see 12), *they gathered them and filled twelve baskets with the pieces of the five barley loaves* (13). They have more food *after* the miracle than they had *before* it!

3. – The reaction (14-15)

It looks like significant numbers of people, as they watch Jesus in action and eat their fill, are looking ahead to the messianic banquet and saying *Surely this is the Prophet who is to come into the world* (14). They are thinking of Deuteronomy 18:15 as well as Isaiah 25:6-8.

But Jesus knows that the common understanding of the Messiah is of a political king who would throw the occupying Romans out of Israel. So *Jesus, knowing that they intended to come and make him king by force, withdrew again to a mountain by himself* (15).

By telling us the people's reaction John is surely asking us, his readers, how *we* are going to react to this astonishing sign of Jesus.

Sign B. Jesus walks on Lake Galilee (6:16-24)

By telling us about this miracle immediately after the feeding of the 5,000 John is following Matthew and Mark (see Matt 14:22 and Mark 6:45). Jesus walking on the lake is almost unique in being a miracle with only the disciples present: he is training them to recognise who he is.

1. – The situation (16-18)

As the disciples, without Jesus, begin rowing across Lake Galilee, *a strong wind was blowing and the waters grew rough* (18). Despite what many commentators say, this is not a storm. The disciples are not in danger, but they do have their work cut out to make progress on their journey.

2. – The miracle (19-21)

After some time the disciples are terrified because they see *Jesus approaching the boat, walking on the water* (19b). Most of us reading this know the story already, so we are not surprised, let alone frightened.

But Jesus is able to walk on the surface of the water: apparently he has suspended the downward drag of gravity. This should stop us in our tracks and make us ask ourselves the question *Who is this man?*

Jesus says to the disciples *It is I; don't be afraid* (20b). He may just mean *It's me* but the words in the Greek are *I am*, which is the name God used when revealing himself to Moses from the burning bush (see Exod 3:14). Is Jesus revealing himself here to his disciples as God (see also Job 9:8)?

3. – The reaction (22-24)

John doesn't tell us anything about how the disciples react after they have welcomed Jesus into the boat. Instead he concentrates on the crowds, who have missed the second sign but experienced the first.

So they want to find Jesus: they are curious to know more about this extraordinary man. Perhaps they are hoping for a repeat of the signs they have seen. But they have questions, too.

The two miracles at the beginning of Section Three are signs pointing the disciples to the identity of Jesus. His feeding of a large crowd, a preview of the messianic banquet, points to his being the Messiah; his walking on Lake Galilee points to his being the Creator. Jesus is training his disciples to recognise who he is.

He is training us, too.

Three blocks

John has already told us that the time for celebrating the Jewish Passover is near (see chapter 6:4). This was a time when people would be thinking not only of the Passover events but also of God's generosity to their nation subsequently in the wilderness.

When Israel were hungry he gave them bread (or manna); when they were thirsty he gave them water; when they needed light he provided what they needed through a pillar of fire (see Exodus chapter 16:4; 17:6; 13:21).

Now, in the three blocks of Section Three, Jesus claims to be the fulfilment of those three gifts: he is the bread of life, the source of water and the light of the world.

Block X. Jesus: the bread of life (6:25-71)

We hear Jesus teaching here as he reacts to the questions and arguments the crowds put to him. But Jesus is not only teaching about *himself*; he is also talking about *them*.

And so each step of the way he tells them how they should be responding to him.

1. – His diagnosis (25-34)

Jesus tells the crowds that they are superficial in their response: they are looking for him *not because you saw the signs I performed but because you ate the loaves and had your fill* (26). They think they will find satisfaction in *stuff.*

So he begs them to change: *Do not work for food that spoils, but for food that endures to eternal life, which the Son of Man will give you* (27a).

And now comes the proof that Jesus' diagnosis is accurate, because the crowds ask *What sign then will you give that we may see it?* (30a) Jesus replies that *he* is the sign. He explains that *it is not Moses who has given you the bread from heaven, but it is my Father who gives you the true bread from heaven* (32b).

So Jesus is not talking about manna when he says *the bread of God is the bread that comes down from heaven and gives life to the world* (33). He is talking about himself, and telling the crowds how they should respond to him: *The work of God is this: to believe in the one he has sent* (29).

And now Jesus spells that out.

2. – His claim (35-48)

I am the bread of life (35a). All of us need bread to keep us alive: Jesus is saying that if we are to experience the life of God in our lives, we need *him.*

But Jesus is claiming more here. He talks about God the Father *giving* him people: *All those the Father gives me will come to me, and whoever comes to me I will never drive away* (37). At the beginning of his Gospel John has already said something very like this (see chapter 1:12-13), and Jesus made the same point in his conversation with Nicodemus (see chapter 3:3).

Some leading Jews start to *grumble about him* (41) because of his claims. But Jesus repeats both of them: *No one can come to me unless the Father who sent me draws them* (44a) and, once again, unmistakeably, *I am the bread of life* (48).

In this part of the discussion Jesus is also making clear how he wants people to respond. He wants us to believe in him, *for my Father's will is that everyone who looks to the Son and believes in him shall have eternal life, and I will raise them up at the last day* (40; see also 46,47).

We come to Jesus by believing in him (see 35).

3. – His explanation (49-59)

By this time in the discussion we may already be in the synagogue in Capernaum (see 59).

Jesus compares the manna God gave Israel in the wilderness with what he calls *the living bread* (51). All the people who ate manna eventually died (see 49), but, talking about himself, Jesus says that *whoever eats this bread will live for ever* (51).

And now he explains how he is using the word *bread*: *This bread is my flesh, which I will give for the life of the world* (51b). I assume that none of those listening understood what Jesus meant by giving his life for the life of the world; but as we look back on this conversation it is impossible to read those words without thinking of the cross. His death means life for the world.

When his listeners start discussing *How can this man give us his flesh to eat?* (52b), Jesus chooses to keep using this shocking language: *Whoever eats my flesh and drinks my blood has eternal life* (54a; see also 53,56).

Jesus is explaining what he meant by *believing in him* (see 29) and by *coming to him* (see 35,37). Just as eating something makes it a part of me, so believing in Jesus and coming to Jesus is like taking him into my personality. This is the response that Jesus is looking for from us.

4. – His question (60-71)

Jesus refuses to back down, and he repeats something he has said earlier: *No one can come to me unless the Father has enabled them* (65b; see also 37,44).

This results in many people making the decision to stop following him. This, in turn, prompts Jesus to ask the twelve disciples a question: *You do not want to leave too, do you?* (67)

Simon Peter's answer must have filled Jesus with joy: *Lord, to whom shall we go? You have the words of eternal life. We have come to believe and to know that you are the Holy One of God* (68-69).

Holy One of God is probably another way of saying *Messiah*. Add to that Peter's mention of *believing* and of *eternal life*, and it seems obvious that John has chapter 20:30-31 in mind in recounting this incident.

Jesus knows that Judas Iscariot will betray him (see 64,70-71). But Peter's passionate expression of faith in Jesus is the big story here: the whole chapter has been leading up to this; this is a turning point in the Gospel. This group of disciples have become convinced that Jesus is the Messiah and the bread of life, *and they have believed in him.*

John is wanting us to do the same.

Block Y. Jesus: the source of water (7:1-52)

The feeding of the 5,000 at the start of Section Three took place in March or April, in the lead-up to Passover (see chapter 6:4). Now this part of the section begins *when the Jewish Festival of Tabernacles was near* (2), which happened in September or October.

So when John tells us that *Jesus went around in Galilee* (1), he is summarizing the six months which Mark tells us more about (see Mark chapters 6, 7 and 8).

Jesus' brothers want him to go up to the Feast because, though not believing in him as the Messiah, they think he should put himself out there and show people what he is made of (see 3-5). And the Feast of Tabernacles sounds like a great opportunity.

The reason is that so many people would be in Jerusalem to celebrate God's care for Israel when they were on their journey from Egypt to the Promised Land. During that time, because they were on the move, they had lived in booths or tabernacles.

There were three important ingredients to the Festival. First, everyone built booths which they slept in during the eight nights they were in Jerusalem. Second, there was a procession every day to a spring called Gihon when a priest would fill up a golden jug with water; after the procession got back to the temple the water would be poured out at the altar. And, third, every evening and right through the night, four huge candles erected in the temple would be burning.

This provides vital background for what is to come.

Jesus tells his brothers *You go to the festival. I am not going up to this festival, because my time has not yet fully come* (8). But then, after his brothers have left, he does follow them to Jerusalem (see 10).

1. – Jesus' authority (10-24)

There are a variety of opinions about Jesus, says John. Some say *He is a good man* (12a), while others say *No, he deceives the people* (12b). And when people hear him teaching in the temple courts there is general astonishment: *How did this man get such learning without having been taught?* (15)

Their amazement is because Jesus is teaching with an authority that comes from God (see 16): *Anyone who chooses to do the will of God will find out whether my teaching comes from God or whether I speak on my own* (17).

And now it is Jesus' turn to express surprise: *Has not Moses given you the law? Yet not one of you keeps the law. Why are you trying to kill me?* (19) The response from the crowd is to claim that no one is trying to kill him and to say *You are demon-possessed* (20a).

In defence of his authority Jesus reminds the crowd of how it was permitted to circumcise a baby boy on the Sabbath: *Now if a boy can be circumcised on the Sabbath so that the law of Moses may not be broken, why are you angry with me for healing a man's whole body on the Sabbath?* (23, and see chapter 5:1-9).

So now it is Jesus who is on the attack. He tells them to *stop judging by mere appearances, but instead judge correctly* (24).

2. – Jesus' identity (25-36)

The theme of authority is still an issue here (see 28-29), but now John is showing us that the questions about Jesus' identity are intensifying.

Some people think that the question has already been settled: *Have the authorities really concluded that he is the Messiah?* (26b) But, they reason, this is out of the question: *But we know where this man is from; when the Messiah comes, no one will know where he is from* (27). They are probably basing this on the view that the Messiah's origin would only be known when he was revealed in glory.

When Jesus announces *I am with you for only a short time, and then I am going to the one who sent me* (33), some of the religious leaders wonder if he is talking about leaving Jerusalem so that he can teach Jews living outside of Israel: *Will he go where our people live scattered among the Greeks, and teach the Greeks?* (35b)

Who is this man? Things have reached the point where the identity of Jesus is a major topic of conversation in Jerusalem.

John wants the same to be true for his readers.

3. – Jesus' promise (37-44)

After the people have watched the daily procession from the Gihon Spring to the temple Jesus does two things to make sure that everyone hears him: he stands, and he calls out in a loud voice. And this is his invitation: *Let anyone who is thirsty come to me and drink* (37b).

Imagine the impact in the temple. And now comes Jesus' promise: *Whoever believes in me, as Scripture has said, rivers of living water will flow from within them* (38).

John explains what Jesus is saying: *By this he meant the Spirit, whom those who believed in him were later to receive. Up to that time the Spirit had not been given, since Jesus had not yet been glorified* (39).

Which part of the Old Testament is Jesus thinking of when he says that this promise fulfils Scripture? Among a number of possibilities, God's promise through Ezekiel of the new covenant is a strong contender because Jesus has already alluded to it when talking to Nicodemus (see my comments on chapter 3:3-10):

> *I will sprinkle clean water on you, and you will be clean;*
> *I will cleanse you from all your impurities and from all your idols.*
> *I will give you a new heart and put a new spirit in you;*
> *I will remove from you your heart of stone*
>   *and give you a heart of flesh.*
> *And I will put my Spirit in you and move you to follow my decrees*
>   *and be careful to keep my laws.*
>   (Ezek 36:25-27, but see also Ezek 47:1-11 and Zech 14:8)

The *rivers of living water* (38) are the Holy Spirit flowing from Jesus to believers: he is the source of the water.

Which is why we need to come to him and drink (see 37b).

Jesus' promise here unleashes another burst of opinions about him. Some say he is the Prophet (of Deuteronomy 18:15) and some that he is the Messiah (see 40-41a): in the first century some Jews were of the opinion that these were two different people, while others held that the Prophet *was* the Messiah.

But there are negative views too. Some say *How can the Messiah come from Galilee? Does not Scripture say that the Messiah will come from David's descendants and from Bethlehem, the town where David lived?* (41b-42) They are right about Bethlehem (see Micah 5:2), but wrong in thinking Jesus was born in Galilee.

But the tension is increasing: *Some wanted to seize him, but no one laid a hand on him* (44).

John has already told us that, because of their concern about Jesus, *the chief priests and the Pharisees sent temple guards to arrest him* (32b). Now the guards return and explain that they have not done so because *no one ever spoke the way this man does* (46).

Nicodemus warns his colleagues about rejecting Jesus without evidence: *Does our law condemn a man without first hearing him to find out what he has been doing?* (51)

John is absolutely right when he tells us that *the people were divided because of Jesus* (43).

He wants us to take sides too.

Block Z. Jesus: the light of the world (8:12-59)

What has happened to the story of Jesus and the woman caught in adultery (chapter 7:53 - 8:11)? You will see from your Bible that the manuscript evidence is that this passage was not originally part of John's Gospel. I think this is right, even though I have no doubt that this incident really happened. See the larger commentaries for details.

1. – Jesus' authority (12-30)

We are still at the Feast of Tabernacles: every evening the four huge candles are lit in the temple. And now Jesus says *I am the light of the world. Whoever follows me will never walk in darkness, but will have the light of life* (12b).

Because of the words *of the world* it is hard not to think of what God says to his servant in the servant songs in the prophecy of Isaiah: *It is too small a thing for you to be my servant to restore the tribes of Jacob and bring back those of Israel I have kept. I will also make you a light for the Gentiles, that my salvation may reach to the ends of the earth* (Isa 49:6, and see also John 4:42b).

And now here is Jesus saying *I am the light of the world.*

The Pharisees maintain that Jesus' statement is of no value because he is saying these things on his own authority (see 13). In reply Jesus explains that he is also claiming these things on the authority of his Father: *I am one who testifies for myself; my other witness is the Father, who sent me* (18).

But they don't understand what father Jesus is talking about (see 19,27).

The tension is building: *He spoke these words while teaching in the temple courts near the place where the offerings were put. Yet no one seized him, because his hour had not yet come* (20).

When Jesus says that he is going away, the religious leaders wonder if he means that he is planning to kill himself (see 21-22). But Jesus is on the attack: *I told you that you would die in your sins; if you do not believe that I am he, you will indeed die in your sins* (24).

This is straight talking. But there is something else here too. The words *I am* in Greek could just mean *I am the one I claim to be*; but it could be that Jesus is deliberately using the words *I am* as the name of God again (see my comments on chapter 6:20).

Jesus is still explaining by what authority he is saying all these things: *I have much to say in judgment of you. But he who sent me is trustworthy, and what I have heard from him I tell the world* (26).

And now Jesus combines three crucial elements of his teaching: *When you have lifted up the Son of Man, then you will know that I am he and that I do nothing on my own but speak just what the Father has taught me* (28).

First, he talks again about his identity: he is *the Son of Man* (see my comments on chapter 1:50-51) and the *I am* (see 24).

Second, in saying he will be *lifted up*, Jesus is referring not only to his death but to *how* he will die. *Lifted up* also means *exalted,* but everyone nailed on a cross was *lifted up*, too (see my comments on chapter 3:14).

And third, Jesus is stressing, once again, that his authority comes from his Father.

And there are people listening, says John, to whom this is beginning to make sense: *Even as he spoke, many believed in him* (30).

2. – What Jesus thinks of the crowd (31-47)

Now Jesus tells the crowd some home truths, presumably because their faith in him is the superficial kind we met earlier, in Section One (see chapter 2:23-24).

In verses 31-36 Jesus tells his listeners that they are slaves to sin, because *everyone who sins is a slave to sin* (34). And they can be set free in two ways. First, says Jesus, *you will know the truth, and the truth will set you free* (32). And second, *if the Son sets you free, you will be free indeed* (36).

And of course, that is not two ways of being set free from sin, but one.

In verses 37-40 Jesus tells these would-be disciples that they are not Abraham's children. *I know you are Abraham's descendants* (37a), says Jesus; but because they are not behaving as Abraham would, they have no right to call themselves his children: if they were Abraham's children, they *would do what Abraham did* (39b).

Jesus wants to be absolutely clear: *As it is, you are looking for a way to kill me, a man who has told you the truth that I heard from God. Abraham did not do such things* (40).

In verses 41-47 Jesus tells them that they are the devil's children, because they are acting like the devil. They claim, of course, that God is their Father, but Jesus says *If God were your Father, you would love me, for I have come here from God* (42a).

Instead, says Jesus, *you belong to your father, the devil, and you want to carry out your father's desires* (44a).

They are like the devil in two ways. First, they don't recognise the truth: speaking about the devil, Jesus says that *he is a liar and the father of lies. Yet because I tell the truth, you do not believe me!* (44c-45) And second, just as *the devil was a murderer from the beginning* (44), says Jesus, *you are looking for a way to kill me* (37,40).

This is strong stuff. John has already told us that Jesus can see what is really going on inside people (see chapter 2:25).

So inevitably there is a counter-attack on the part of the crowd.

3. – What the crowd think of Jesus (48-59)

Jesus has brought three accusations against the crowd; now they bring three accusations against him.

Up to now in Section Three there have been voices *for* Jesus and voices *against* Jesus, but now it looks like the reactions are increasingly negative. As we approach the end of the section the opposition is reaching a crescendo.

First, say the crowds, Jesus is *a Samaritan and demon-possessed* (48b). Jesus ignores the Samaritan jibe, and explains that he is not demon-possessed because *I am not seeking glory for myself* (50a). And then he adds these words: *Very truly I tell you, whoever obeys my word will never see death* (51).

This is enough to prompt a second accusation: *Are you greater than our father Abraham? He died, and so did the prophets. Who do you think you are?* (53) How conceited is this man, to believe that he can deliver people from death!

In his reply Jesus returns to the subject of glory (see 50): *If I glorify myself, my glory means nothing. My Father, whom you claim as your God, is the one who glorifies me* (54).

Things are moving fast. Jesus makes an extraordinary claim about Abraham: *Your father Abraham rejoiced at the thought of seeing my day; he saw it and was glad* (56).

The crowd take this literally: what Jesus has just said is impossible because he is hardly of the same generation as Abraham (see 57)!

Imagine heaven holding its breath as Jesus replies. *Very truly I tell you,* he says, which shows that what is coming is incredibly solemn and important: *before Abraham was born, I am!* (58)

If Jesus had said that before Abraham was born, he *was*, that would have been a claim to pre-existence. But in saying *Before Abraham was born, I am*, Jesus is using the name of God for himself (see my comments on chapter 6:20).

He is unmistakeably claiming to be God.

Which, understandably, prompts the third accusation from the crowd: Jesus is a blasphemer. But they don't use words to say this, but stones: *At this, they picked up stones to stone him, but Jesus hid himself, slipping away from the temple grounds* (59).

Section Three has reached its climax. This has all been training for the disciples, as they have watched and listened.

The opposition to Jesus has been growing as more and more people make the decision that he must be done away with. And Jesus has revealed himself to be the bread of life, the source of water and the light of the world.

And God himself.

Learning the Gospel

First, learn the headings in bold: this will not be difficult. (And remember that doing this out loud will make it easier and quicker.)

Second, learn the sub-headings for the signs, which is easy since they are repeated. As you do so you will find yourself remembering some of the details.

Third, turn to the three blocks: learn the sub-headings. I suggest you don't go on to the second block until you are sure you have learnt the sub-headings for the first.

You will find it a help to have arranged with a friend that both of you will learn the order of the events in the section.

It won't take you long to learn this section, despite its length. And if you run through it in your mind once or twice a day, it will soon be in your long-term memory.

Section Three: The Training

Two signs

A. Jesus feeds the 5,000
1. The situation
2. The miracle
3. The reaction

B. Jesus walks on Lake Galilee
1. The situation
2. The miracle
3. The reaction

Three blocks

X. Jesus: the bread of life

1. His diagnosis
2. His claim
3. His explanation
4. His question

Y. Jesus: the source of water

1. Jesus' authority
2. Jesus' identity
3. Jesus' promise

Z. Jesus: the light of the world

1. Jesus' authority
2. What Jesus thinks of the crowd
3. What the crowd think of Jesus

Meeting the Lord

Please remember that John's Gospel is not only there so we can have information about Jesus: it is also there so we can meet him. You can do this on your own or with a friend.

Begin telling the story of the two signs and, as you do so, start talking to Jesus about what he is doing and saying. Ask him to train you, as he was training the disciples.

Then do the same with the three blocks. You won't remember all the details at this point, but talk to Jesus about what you *do* remember. Ask him to help you to keep believing in him as the bread of life; open yourself up to the Holy Spirit in response to Jesus' promise that he is the source of water; invite Jesus to shine into your life as the light of the world.

And worship him because he is *I am*.

If you re-tell some (or all) of Section Three to yourself every day, and turn it into prayer as you do, the Holy Spirit will use his word in your life to give you new joy and peace: you will be getting to know Jesus better.

It makes sense to try the experiment of rediscovering Jesus.

Section Four: The Cost (John 9:1 - 11:57)

Section Three, with all its discussions about Jesus' identity, ended with the decision to stone him for blasphemy. In Section Four the question becomes louder: *Who is this man?* Another major theme in this section is the issue of cost. What will it cost Jesus to enable him to offer men and women eternal life? And what will it cost people who make the decision to believe in him and follow him?

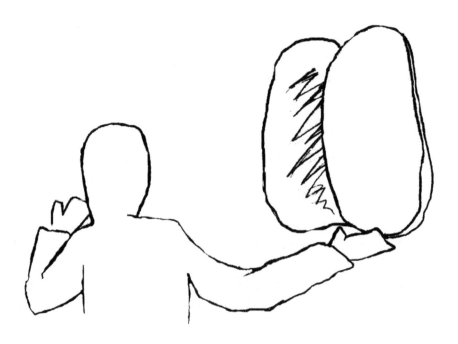

Jesus called in a loud voice,
'Lazarus, come out!'

John 11:43

Enjoying the View

As we would expect, there are two signs and three blocks in Section Four. But in this case only one of the signs is at the beginning of the section.

The reason is not hard to find: it is important to John to provide a chronological account of the Jesus story (see Appendix 1 for more details). The events of chapter 10 took place between the healing of the blind man and the raising of Lazarus, so that's the way John tells the story.

Another thing worth noticing about the two signs in this section is that John takes much longer in the telling of them. The question is: why?

Sign A. Jesus heals a man born blind (9:1-41)

1. The healing (1-12)
2. The investigation (13-34)
3. The decision (35-41)

Block X. Jesus: the good shepherd (10:1-21)

a. The parable (1-6)
b. Jesus is the door (7-10)
b'. Jesus is the shepherd (11-18)
a'. The reaction (19-21)

Block Y. Jesus: who is this man? (10:22-42)

1. Jesus is the Messiah (22-30)
2. Jesus is the Son of God (31-39)

Sign B. Jesus raises Lazarus from death (11:1-44)

1. Trust his plan (1-16)
2. Hear his claim (17-27)
3. See his tears (28-37)
4. Experience his power (38-44)

Block Z. Jesus: this man must die (11:45-57)

1. What Caiaphas says (45-53)
2. What Jesus does (54-57)

Before reading further it would be good to read through the whole section in John's Gospel. As you do you will notice that the issue of Jesus' identity is at the forefront.

Notice, too, how John points us to what Jesus' mission from his Father will cost him, and to what it costs others to follow Jesus.

And as you see Jesus in action and hear him teach, please take the opportunity to pray and to worship.

Unpacking the Content

Sign A. Jesus heals a man born blind (9:1-41)

Giving the sign this heading could be misleading. The healing takes place in verse 7: there is a lot of chapter 9 still to come!

We will notice two other elements which are important to John. The first is the continuing opposition of the religious leaders, and the second is the issue of *spiritual* blindness.

And of course these two ingredients are linked.

1. – The healing (1-12)

As he went along, he saw a man blind from birth (1). This is like the headline to the chapter: John is underlining that this man didn't *become* blind, but *was born* blind.

The disciples' question is about whose fault the man's blindness is (see 2), but Jesus stresses that *this happened so that the works of God might be displayed in him* (3). Since he knows that he is about to heal the blind man, Jesus is claiming that his work of power will be a work of God.

And, because he is about to transform the life of a man who has always lived in physical darkness, Jesus reminds his disciples *I am the light of the world* (5b, see also chapter 8:12).

After smearing some mud on the blind man's eyes, Jesus tells him to go and wash in the Pool of Siloam. Why does Jesus use this method of healing, when he could have just said the word? Of course we don't know. But maybe he, like John, wants the *meaning* of the pool's name – *Sent* (see 7) – to remind us of something.

Jesus often refers in his teaching to *the Father who sent me* (see chapter 5:24,36,37,38; 6:38,39,44,57; 7:18,28,29; 8:16,18,29). And he has just said it again in chapter 9 (see 4). Jesus is on a mission and he doesn't want us to forget it.

How much emotion there must be alongside the words *So the man went and washed, and came home seeing* (7b)! This extraordinary miracle has changed everything for this man.

John tells us how, understandably, the healed man's neighbours have difficulty in believing *their* eyes (see 8-9). But the man is more than willing to tell his story: *The man they call Jesus made some mud and put it on my eyes. He told me to go to Siloam and wash. So I went and washed, and then I could see* (11).

That could be the end of the story. But there is more to come.

2. – The investigation (13-34)

This is the Pharisees wanting to discover what has really happened at the Pool of Siloam. But John tells us why they are so determined: *the day on which Jesus had made the mud and opened the man's eyes was a Sabbath* (14). This has already been an issue with Jesus' signs (see my comments on chapter 5:9-12).

The Pharisees' investigation has three parts.

Part One sees them interrogating the healed man (see 13-17). The man tells his story again (see 15b), but the fact that a blind man can now see is irrelevant to them: *This man is not from God, for he does not keep the Sabbath* (16).

The Pharisees are being ironic in verse 17: they still don't believe that a healing has taken place at all (see 18). When asked what he makes of Jesus, the man has no hesitation: *He is a prophet* (17b).

Part Two of the investigation is a cross-examination of the healed man's parents (see 18-23). When the Pharisees ask them to explain what has happened (see 19), their answer is very careful. They admit that this is their son and that he was blind from birth (see 20): *But how he can see now, or who opened his eyes, we don't know. Ask him. He is of age; he will speak for himself* (21).

The man's parents are so wary because they are afraid of the religious leaders, *who already had decided that anyone who acknowledged that Jesus was the Messiah would be put out of the synagogue* (22b).

Part Three of the Pharisees' investigation (see 24-34) sees them trying to get the healed man to break down under cross-questioning.

But the man is not giving an inch. When they say Jesus must be a sinner, he replies *Whether he is a sinner or not, I don't know. One thing I do know. I was blind but now I see!* (25) It's as if he's saying to the Pharisees *Get round that!*

Even though he must know that he is in danger of being thrown out of the synagogue (see 22), the healed man is so enthusiastic about Jesus that, when asked to repeat the details of the healing, he resorts to sarcasm: *I have told you already and you did not listen. Why do you want to hear it again? Do you want to become his disciples too?* (27)

And we should notice here that the implication of that last question is that this man has become a Jesus disciple himself.

The Pharisees have obviously noticed that too: *You are this fellow's disciple! We are disciples of Moses! We know that God spoke to Moses, but as for this fellow, we don't even know where he comes from* (28-29).

It is worth reading the whole of the man's magnificent reply in verses 30-33: it is an impassioned defence of Jesus. He finishes like this: *Nobody has ever heard of opening the eyes of a man born blind. If this man were not from God, he could do nothing* (32-33).

The Pharisees have hit a brick wall: they have had enough. *You were steeped in sin at birth; how dare you lecture us!* (34a)

And then, says John, *they threw him out* (34b). This is not just throwing him out of the room, though doubtless they did that too. This is excommunication.

This means much more than that the man will not be able to go to synagogue on the Sabbath: he will be excluded from the social life of the community. This is harsh punishment.

That is what it costs this man to start following Jesus.

3. – The decision (35-41)

The healed man has already made *his*. But John tells us this part of the story to explain that there are two possible reactions to this Jesus sign.

And everyone has to make their own mind up.

The first reaction is to believe in Jesus, which is something John stresses throughout his Gospel (see chapter 20:30-31). Jesus searches for the man and asks him the question *Do you believe in the Son of Man?* (35)

The man's reply *Who is he, sir?* (36a) shows that he knows Jesus is talking about the glorious Son of Man (see my comments on chapter 1:50-51, and also Dan 7:13-14).

Jesus' answer is beautiful: *You have now seen him; in fact, he is the one speaking with you* (37). Not only is Jesus introducing himself as the Son of Man: he is also telling a man born blind that he can *see* him.

There is no hesitation on the man's part: *Lord, I believe* (38). And he falls to his knees to worship Jesus.

Since his healing he has been on a journey: he has called Jesus *a man* (11), *a prophet* (17), someone *from God* (33), and now *Lord* (38).

It's as if John is asking *us* the question *Where are you on the journey?*

The second reaction is to reject Jesus. He spells it out: *For judgment I have come into this world, so that the blind will see and those who see will become blind* (39). Jesus is talking about spiritual blindness.

If we admit that we *can't* see and don't understand lots about God and the meaning of life, Jesus will open our eyes (which he has done for the healed man in the course of the chapter).

But if we insist that we *can* see, as the Pharisees do (see 40), we will become more and more unable to understand anything at all.

As Jesus says: *If you were blind, you would not be guilty of sin; but now that you claim you can see, your guilt remains* (41).

Every one of us has a decision to make.

Block X. Jesus: the good shepherd (10:1-21)

If we see this passage as a simple example of mirror linking, it will help us to understand what we are reading, and to remember it too.

a. – The parable (1-6)

Jesus introduces three important elements in his story.

First, the sheep (see 3-5); second, the gate (see 1-3); and third, the shepherd (2-4).

Sometimes someone climbs into the sheepfold, avoiding the gate: Jesus says they are *a thief and a robber* (1), and then calls them *a stranger*, because the sheep refuse to follow them (5).

There is a relationship between the shepherd and the sheep. The sheep *listen to his voice* (3), *know his voice* and *follow him* (4), and they belong to the shepherd: they are *his own sheep* (3).

I called this parable a *story*; John, more accurately, calls it a *figure of speech* (6a). What is more important is that Jesus begins it by making clear who it is for: *Very truly I tell you Pharisees...* (1). And John ends the paragraph by explaining that *the Pharisees did not understand what he was telling them* (6b).

So Jesus starts to explain himself.

b. – Jesus is the gate (7-10)

This seems like a very weird image until we realise that there was usually no gate in a sheep pen, but instead just one gap in the wall. After bringing his sheep into the fold as night was falling, the shepherd would sleep lying down across the entrance in order to prevent the sheep from leaving.

So the shepherd could truly say *I am the gate* (7).

In calling himself the gate Jesus compares himself with *thieves and robbers* (8). It seems inescapable that he is referring to the Pharisees and the other religious leaders of Israel, who neglect the people they are supposed to be looking after. They are in it for what they can get out of it: they come only *to steal and kill and destroy* (10a).

Jesus is quite different: *I am the gate; whoever enters through me will be saved. They will come in and go out, and find pasture* (9). Jesus is still using sheep imagery here, but now he drops it completely: *I have come that they may have life, and have it to the full* (10b, and see chapter 20:31).

b'. – Jesus is the shepherd (11-18)

Jesus says it plainly: *I am the good shepherd* (11a,14a).

The background here may be the prophecy of Ezekiel in the Old Testament. Using the image of sheep to talk about his people, God says *I will place over them one shepherd, my servant David, and he will tend them; he will tend them and be their shepherd* (Ezek 34:23). This promise was understood to refer to the Messiah, the Son of David and the shepherd-king, who would one day come to bring God's blessing on earth.

It's like Jesus is saying *I'm fulfilling that promise.*

The first time Jesus says *I am the good shepherd* (11a), he goes on to talk about his uniqueness. He compares himself with the hired hand whom he describes like this: *When he sees the wolf coming, he abandons the sheep and runs away* (12b).

Jesus is still talking about the Pharisees (see 6) and the other religious leaders of Israel, who are not taking their responsibility seriously. They are just doing a job: *The man runs away because he is a hired hand and cares nothing for the sheep* (13). But Jesus is quite different.

The second time Jesus says *I am the good shepherd* (14a), he explains that the sheep of God's people Israel are not the whole story: *I have other sheep that are not of this sheepfold. I must bring them also. They too will listen to my voice, and there shall be one flock and one shepherd* (16).

Jesus is talking about Gentiles also coming to know God. He is thinking back to promises such as the one we have already looked at (see my comments on chapter 8:12), when God was speaking to his servant: *It is too small a thing for you to be my servant to restore the tribes of Jacob and bring back those of Israel I have kept. I will also make you a light for the Gentiles, that my salvation may reach to the ends of the earth* (Isa 49:6; see also Isa 42:1,4).

And he is looking forward to the perfected church in heaven, made up of Jews and Gentiles who have come home to God through the work of Jesus the shepherd (see Rev 5:9; 7:9).

And what *is* the work of Jesus the shepherd? Both times when he says the words *I am the good shepherd*, Jesus goes on to say that *the good shepherd lays down his life for the sheep* (11b,15b).

He tells us four things here about his death, all of which tell us what it cost Jesus to be the shepherd-saviour. And all of them may prompt us to imitate the healed blind man of chapter 9, and worship Jesus (see chapter 9:38).

So what does Jesus say about his death?

First, it's voluntary. Talking about his life, Jesus says *No one takes it from me, but I lay it down of my own accord* (18a). He is *choosing* to go to his death.

Second, it's substitutionary. That means that Jesus dies in the place of and so for the sake of others: instead of just laying down his life, he lays it down *for the sheep* (11b,15b).

Third, it's victorious. The end of Jesus' life is not the end of Jesus' life: *The reason my Father loves me is that I lay down my life – only to take it up again* (17). And he repeats it: *I have authority to lay it down and authority to take it up again* (18b). Jesus' resurrection proclaims his victory.

And fourth, it's planned. Jesus tells us: *This command I received from my Father* (18c). It always *was* the plan of God. Jesus' death is not going to be a random tragedy, but the means by which God saves sinners (see chapter 3:16).

Jesus doesn't use the word *cross* here, though he has already alluded to it (see chapter 3:14; 8:28). But the message is one Jesus wants everyone to understand: his death on the cross is what it cost him to save us, and it is voluntary, substitutionary, victorious and planned.

It's a message which should cause us to thank the good shepherd.

a'. – The reaction (19-21)

The religious leaders *who heard these words were again divided* (19), John tells us.

It looks like most of them continue to say that Jesus is demon-possessed (see 20, and also chapter 7:20; 8:48,52). But others are impressed by the healing miracle of the previous chapter: *These are not the sayings of a man possessed by a demon. Can a demon open the eyes of the blind?* (21)

John is wanting us to make up our own minds about Jesus.

Block Y. Jesus: who is this man? (10:22-42)

We are at the Feast of Dedication (see 22), which was a celebration of the reconsecration of the temple in 164BC after it had been defiled by the Syrian Antiochus Epiphanes.

And it seems like the big topic of conversation on the street is the identity of Jesus.

1. – Jesus is the Messiah (22-30)

So the question comes from some in the crowd: *How long will you keep us in suspense? If you are the Messiah, tell us plainly* (24).

The answer from Jesus is unambiguous: *I did tell you, but you do not believe* (25a). The reason they don't believe is that *you are not my sheep* (26). But people *should* believe that he is the Messiah because of the works hc docs (see 25b), which fulfil such prophecies as Isaiah 35:5-6.

And now, talking about his relationship with those who do believe in him, Jesus says *I give them eternal life, and they shall never perish; no one will snatch them out of my hand* (28). And then he adds *My Father, who has given them to me, is greater than all; no one can snatch them out of my Father's hand* (29).

So Jesus says that those who believe in him are secure in *my hand* (28b) and secure in *my Father's hand* (29b). This is astonishing use of language. There is only one conclusion to draw, and Jesus draws it: *I and the Father are one* (30).

This is the climax of Jesus' argument that he is the Messiah. But there is more to come.

2. – Jesus is the Son of God (31-39)

Jesus' statement *I and the Father are one* (30) results in an immediate decision to stone him (see 31). When Jesus asks the reason, they explain that it is *for blasphemy, because you, a mere man, claim to be God* (33b).

They have got the message. And they don't like it.

Now, quoting from Psalm 82:6, Jesus reminds them of a common belief in the first century that, at the giving of the Law at Mount Sinai, God had said to his people *You are 'gods'*. The rest of Psalm 82:6 has God saying *You are all sons of the Most High.*

So, says Jesus, how can they accuse him of blasphemy for claiming to be the Son of God (see 36)?

But Jesus is not asking them to accept him as God's Son because of a verse in Psalm 82. Instead he points his hearers to his actions: *Do not believe me unless I do the works of my Father. But if I do them, even though you do not believe me, believe the works* (37-38a).

And if they *do* believe the works, they will *know and understand that the Father is in me, and I in the Father* (38b).

Jesus' insistence on his intimate relationship with God his Father means *they tried to seize him, but he escaped their grasp* (39).

But opposition is not the only reaction to Jesus: there is another possibility. Jesus crosses over the River Jordan to the place where John the Baptist had baptised (see 40). Seeing him, some people remember what John had said: *Though John never performed a sign, all that John said about this man was true* (41b).

So, says John the Gospel-writer, *in that place many believed in Jesus* (42).

Sign B. Jesus raises Lazarus from death (11:1-44)

Have you noticed how John takes much more time to tell us about Jesus' signs here in Section Four than he did in earlier sections?

Perhaps he sees Jesus healing a man blind from birth and Jesus raising a dead man to life as being more significant than the earlier signs in his Gospel.

What is certainly true is this: if we are already familiar with this miracle, we need to try to think ourselves into the situation and so experience its power again.

Then we will meet Jesus. Four scenes will help us to do that.

1. – Trust his plan (1-16)

Lazarus is ill at home in Bethany, and Mary and Martha, his sisters, ask Jesus to come and heal him (see 1 and 3).

The shock is that Jesus, after hearing that his friend is ill, *stayed where he was two more days* (6b). In fact John makes the shock all the greater: verses 5 and 6 are one sentence in the Greek, resulting in this: *Now Jesus loved Martha and her sister and Lazarus, so when he heard that Lazarus was ill, he stayed where he was two more days* (5-6).

In other words, Jesus not going immediately to heal Lazarus is an expression of his love.

There is something else going on here too. Jesus is sure that *this illness will not end in death. No, it is for God's glory so that God's Son may be glorified through it* (4).

So Jesus' plan is not simply that Lazarus will live. What happens in Bethany will be *a sign* which will bring him glory.

And there is another ingredient in this plan. After the disciples have taken literally Jesus' comments about Lazarus being asleep (see 11-13), he spells it out for them: *Lazarus is dead, and for your sake I am glad I was not there, so that you may believe* (14b-15a).

The divine plan is that we recognise who Jesus is and believe in him, which is why John wrote his Gospel (see chapter 20:30-31).

So Jesus decides to go to Bethany: now that Lazarus is dead the plan can be fulfilled.

2. – Hear his claim (17-27)

John tells us that on Jesus' arrival Lazarus had already been dead for four days (see 17). This is important: many Jews in the first century believed that the spirit of a dead person left the body after *three* days.

Martha comes out to meet Jesus. She knows her stuff: *If you had been here, my brother would not have died. But I know that even now God will give you whatever you ask* (21-22). And when Jesus tells her that Lazarus will rise to life, she answers confidently that *I know he will rise again in the resurrection at the last day* (24).

And now comes Jesus' claim: *I am the resurrection and the life* (25a). He has the authority to give people life (see chapter 5:21) because resurrection and life are *in him*.

So Jesus continues: *The one who believes in me will live, even though they die; and whoever lives by believing in me will never die* (25b-26).

His claim has become an invitation. If we trust in Jesus, death is not the end, so it's not really death at all: we will be more alive than we have ever been.

When Jesus asks Martha if she believes this, her answer is Yes: *I believe that you are the Messiah, the Son of God, who is to come into the world* (27).

John wants us to hear Jesus' claim, and to decide to believe in him.

3. – See his tears (28-37)

Mary comes to see Jesus and says exactly what her sister had said earlier (32, see also 21). And they bring him to Lazarus' tomb.

Jesus wept (35).

One reason he cries is love. The people standing around say *See how he loved him!* (36) It's not difficult to see the love of Jesus when you see him interacting with people in the Gospels.

The second reason is anger. When Jesus sees people weeping at the tomb, *he was deeply moved in spirit and troubled* (33b). Instead of *deeply moved* a better translation would be *outraged*.

Jesus is angry at what sin has done to our world. It's not meant to be like this: we're not supposed to have funerals; the word *bereavement* shouldn't be in our dictionaries. Humankind's rebellion against God has resulted in our world being spoilt.

Which is why the Word became flesh (see chapter 1:14).

4. – Experience his power (38-44)

When Martha is unhappy about the stone being rolled away from the entrance to the tomb (see 38-39), Jesus mentions his plan again: *Did I not tell you that if you believe, you will see the glory of God?* (40)

After the stone has been taken away, Jesus prays to his Father *for the benefit of the people standing here, that they may believe that you sent me* (see 41-42). Believing in Jesus is mentioned several times in this chapter (see 15, 25-27, 40, 42): this is how John wants us to respond.

Now Jesus calls out at the top of his voice *Lazarus, come out!* (43b) And then we read what happens: *The dead man came out, his hands and feet wrapped with strips of linen, and a cloth round his face* (44a).

This is the power of Jesus. We should be staggered by this miracle. When Jesus talks to people who have died, they obey him. And this is because of who he is: he is the resurrection and the life.

And to us, who have not yet died, Jesus is issuing an invitation to believe in him. The message could not be clearer.

But for Jesus, there is a price to pay.

Block Z. Jesus: this man must die (11:45-57)

Some believe in Jesus, says John, but others go to tip off the Pharisees about what Jesus has been up to (see 45-46).

1. – What Caiaphas says (45-53)

The Jewish Council is in emergency session (see 47a). It is fascinating to see that they accept that Jesus is doing miracles: *Here is this man performing many signs* (47b).

But there is real concern as to what this could lead to: if Jesus becomes too popular the Romans might decide *to take away both our temple and our nation* (48b).

But the high priest has the solution to the problem. Caiaphas says *You know nothing at all! You do not realise that it is better for you that one man die for the people than that the whole nation perish* (49b-50).

In the first century many believed that the high priest was also a prophet, who sometimes brought a message from God. Now John tells us that, when Caiaphas said Jesus would die for the nation, *he prophesied* (51).

So without realising it, Caiaphas is saying that Jesus will die for the sake of others. He is confirming what Jesus himself said earlier in this section when describing himself as the good shepherd (see chapter 10:11).

And so the religious leaders are more determined than ever to do away with Jesus (see 53, also chapter 5:18; 8:59).

This is the price that Jesus will pay.

2. – What Jesus does (54-57)

John explains that this decision of the religious elite is the reason Jesus pulls back out of the public eye: *Therefore Jesus no longer moved about publicly...* (54a).

People who have travelled to Jerusalem to prepare for the Passover Feast *kept looking for Jesus* (56).

But the religious leaders want to arrest him (see 57).

Learning the Gospel

You may be thinking it will be harder to learn this part of the Gospel because the two signs are not at the beginning of the section. But it really isn't hard at all.

Start, as always, by learning the headings in bold; then go on to learn the sub-headings. Then, as you think yourself through Section Four, you will find yourself remembering all kinds of details.

The people who find it hard to learn a section of John's Gospel are the people who don't try! And it is a wise decision to arrange with a friend that you will both try this experiment.

Section Four: The Cost

Sign A. Jesus heals a man born blind
1. The healing
2. The investigation
3. The decision

Block X. Jesus: the good shepherd
a. The parable
b. Jesus is the door
b'. Jesus is the shepherd
a'. The reaction

Block Y. Jesus: who is this man?
1. Jesus is the Messiah
2. Jesus is the Son of God

Sign B. Jesus raises Lazarus from death
1. Trust his plan
2. Hear his claim
3. See his tears
4. Experience his power

Block Z. Jesus: this man must die
1. What Caiaphas says
2. What Jesus does

Meeting the Lord

As you run through the first sign in your mind (or with a friend), talk to Jesus about what he is doing and about the example of the healed man under cross-examination by the Pharisees.

Then pray through Block X, thanking Jesus for being the door and the shepherd. Thank him for whatever you can remember from the passage about his death.

And so on through the whole section.

I am praying for you that, as you re-tell Section Four of John's Gospel as part of the John experiment, you will rediscover Jesus.

Section Five: The Judgment (John 12:1-50)

We saw it in Section Four: at the same time as the religious leaders have been getting more and more determined to end his life, Jesus has been explaining the meaning of his death. Now, in Section Five, we witness the end of Jesus' public ministry. From chapter 13 onwards he will focus his attention on his disciples, so in this section we will hear Jesus' final message for the crowds, which includes a warning of judgment.

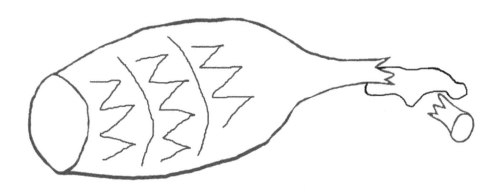

Then Mary took about half a litre of pure nard,
an expensive perfume;
she poured it on Jesus' feet
and wiped his feet with her hair.
And the house was filled
with the fragrance of the perfume.

John 12:3

Enjoying the View

Two signs

A. The anointing in Bethany (12:1-11)

   1. What Mary does (1-3)
   2. How Judas reacts (4-6)
   3. What Jesus says (7-8)

B. The arrival in Jerusalem (12:12-19)

   1. The arrival (12-13)
   2. The meaning (14-15)
   3. The reaction (16-19)

Three blocks

X. The decision (12:20-36)

   1. Jesus (20-26)
   2. The Father (27-33)
   3. The crowd (34-36)

Y. The rejection (12:37-43)

   1. The surprise (37)
   2. The explanation (38-41)
   3. The reaction (42-43)

Z. The invitation (12:44-50)

   1. The necessity of faith (44-46)
   2. The certainty of judgment (47-48)
   3. The message of the Son (49-50)

Section Five is short. The two signs – both at the beginning of the section this time – point to the identity of Jesus and to his death.

The three blocks are like a summary of Jesus' ministry. In the first block a signal prompts him to announce that he is now going to the cross; in the second block John explains the reason why Jesus faces so much opposition; and in the third block Jesus issues a final invitation to believe in him and so receive eternal life.

I suggest you take time to read through chapter 12. As you do, imagine the scene each step of the way and try to think yourself into how Jesus may be feeling.

And please talk to him and worship him: the John experiment is not only about information. It's about encounter too.

Unpacking the Content

Two signs

Sign A. The anointing in Bethany (12:1-11)

1. – What Mary does (1-3)

This is a very unusual interruption to a dinner party!

Lazarus and his two sisters have been invited, as has Jesus (see 2). *Then Mary took about half a litre of pure nard, an expensive perfume; she poured it on Jesus' feet and wiped his feet with her hair* (3a).

Nard was exclusive perfume because of its price, and Mary doesn't stint on its use. This shows how much she loves Jesus, and that she is not afraid of showing it. And she makes it even clearer by wiping his feet with her hair.

This will have surely stopped all the conversation. And John can still remember the smell: *the house was filled with the fragrance of the perfume* (3b).

2. – How Judas reacts (4-6)

The silence is broken by Judas Iscariot, who, John reminds us, is *one of his disciples* (4a): *Why wasn't this perfume sold and the money given to the poor? It was worth a year's wages* (5).

But John knows, as he looks back on the dinner party in Bethany, what Judas' real motivation was: if the perfume had been sold he could have stolen the money for himself (see 6).

And John takes care to remind us of what disciple Judas will do to Jesus: he *was later to betray him* (4).

3. – What Jesus says (7-8)

Leave her alone, Jesus says to Judas (7a). And then he explains that Mary's original plan had been to save the nard *for the day of my burial* (7b).

But clearly she has decided to use it now, either because she just wants to express her love to Jesus, or because she senses that the time for Jesus' burial is not far away. It is probably a combination of both.

In any case, says Jesus, *you will always have the poor among you, but you will not always have me* (8). Of course we should help the poor; but at this moment what Mary has done is absolutely the right thing to do.

This first sign in Section Five points to the fact that Jesus is soon to die, *and knows it* (see 7). And that our reponse to him should be to pour out our lives in love to him.

Before he moves on to the second sign, John tells us that there are still very different reactions to Jesus. There is so much public interest in Lazarus, *whom he had raised from the dead* (9b), that the chief priests decide not only to get rid of Jesus but *made plans to kill Lazarus as well* (10).

But at the same time John can record positive responses to Jesus: because of the Lazarus story *many of the Jews were going over to Jesus and believing in him* (11).

John is providing us with yet another opportunity to decide which group we are going to belong to.

Sign B. The arrival in Jerusalem (12:12-19)

1. – The arrival (12-13)

The great crowd (see 12) who are in Jerusalem to celebrate the Passover Feast come out to welcome Jesus. They arm themselves with palm branches (13a), which were a symbol of victory and kingship: messianic expectation is running high.

This is all the more evident if instead of looking at the crowds we listen to them. They are quoting from Psalm 118 as they shout *Hosanna! Blessed is he who comes in the name of the Lord!* (Ps 118:25a,26a), but the significant thing is what they *add* to this: *Blessed is the king of Israel!*

This last exclamation is not a quotation from Scripture but an expression of messianic fervour. They are clearly hoping and expecting that Jesus is a political Messiah who will deliver Israel from Roman occupation (see also chapter 6:14-15 and chapter 1:49).

2. – The meaning (14-15)

John explains what is happening here by reference to the Old Testament prophet Zechariah, who wrote *Do not be afraid, daughter Zion; see, your king is coming, seated on a donkey's colt* (15, quoting Zech 9:9). Most first-century Jews would have said that this was about the coming of the Messiah.

So when *Jesus found a young donkey and sat upon it* (14), this is a very deliberate act on Jesus' part. Whenever Jesus went anywhere in Israel on land, it was always on foot. This is the only exception.

Jesus has decided to fulfil Zechariah's prophecy: it is as if he is riding into Jerusalem holding up a huge placard saying *I am the Messiah!*

It's like he's saying *Crown me or kill me!*

3. – The reaction (16-19)

Actually John records three reactions for us.

First there is the reaction of the disciples: *Only after Jesus was glorified did they realise that these things had been written about him* (16b).

The second reaction is the enthusiasm of the crowd who had been there when Jesus had raised Lazarus from death: they *continued to spread the word* (17b), which, in turn, results in even more people wanting to satisfy their curiosity about Jesus (see 18).

And, third, there is the reaction of the Pharisees. They clearly feel they are making no progress in their attempts to derail Jesus: *See, this is getting us nowhere!* (19b)

The last thing the Pharisees say about Jesus is *Look how the whole world has gone after him!* (19b) Of course this is just a figure of speech, but the irony is that they are more right than they know.

What happens next is going to confirm that.

Three blocks

As we move into the rest of the chapter, let's remember that these are the last words that Jesus will say in public.

Block X. The decision (12:20-36)

1. – Jesus (20-26)

Through the Gospel so far Jesus has said on a number of occasions that it is not yet the right time. Now he says that *the hour has come for the Son of Man to be glorified* (23). In other words: it is time for him to be *lifted up* on the cross (see my comments on chapter 3:14).

How does Jesus know that it is time to make this decision?

The answer to that question is that *some Greeks* (20) have found Philip and told him *We would like to see Jesus* (21b). It is hearing about this that convinces Jesus that the time has come.

We have already seen that Jesus, as the light of the world, is very aware of God's words to his servant in the prophecy of Isaiah: *It is too small a thing for you to be my servant to restore the tribes of Jacob and bring back those of Israel I have kept. I will also make you a light for the Gentiles, that my salvation may reach to the ends of the earth* (Isa 49:6).

The Greeks John mentions are Gentiles, but sympathetic to the Jewish faith: they are *among those who went up to worship at the festival* (20). So when Jesus hears that *Gentiles* are wanting to come to him it is like God his Father is firing a starting gun.

The Pharisees had been right: *the whole world has gone after him* (19). It is time for Jesus to go to the cross.

So Jesus immediately explains the meaning of his death: *Very truly I tell you, unless a grain of wheat falls to the ground and dies, it remains only a single seed. But if it dies, it produces many seeds* (24). The message is clear: by his death Jesus will give life to many who decide to follow him.

And now Jesus explains what following him involves: *Anyone who loves their life will lose it, while anyone who hates their life in this world will keep it for eternal life* (25). I cannot be a follower of Jesus if I am more preoccupied with looking after myself than I am with loving and serving him.

Jesus wants to help us make the decision to become a disciple: *Whoever serves me must follow me; and where I am, my servant also will be* (26a). And now the greatest encouragement of all: *My Father will honour the one who serves me* (26b).

This should make us catch our breath. If we commit ourselves to serving Jesus, God the Father will *honour* us!

So, because of the Greeks wanting to come to him, Jesus knows that this is the moment to actively be moving towards his cross.

2. – The Father (27-33)

The thought of the cross is weighing heavily on Jesus: *Now my soul is troubled* (27a). But he is not going to run away because *it was for this very reason I came to this hour* (27b).

Jesus sees the centrality of the cross: he came to die.

And because he knows that his death will bring glory to God, Jesus says *Father, glorify your name!* (28a)

Now we learn of the Father's decision, as a voice from heaven announces *I have glorified it, and will glorify it again* (28b). God the Father is always committed to bringing glory to his name (see, for example, chapter 11:4).

Jesus explains that three things will happen when he dies. First, the world will be judged: *now is the time for judgment on this world* (31a). If people reject what Jesus is doing for them on the cross, then judgment is all that awaits them.

Second, *the prince of this world will be driven out* (31b). Satan is like a prince, with power over human beings because he can accuse them: but when Jesus has paid the price for the sins of the world, Satan's accusations have no basis.

And, third, as Jesus is exalted in his death on the cross, he will attract people from all ethnic backgrounds: *And I, when I am lifted up from the earth, will draw all people to myself* (32). And John explains that Jesus says this *to show the kind of death he was going to die* (33).

Way back in verse 23 Jesus had again referred to himself as *the Son of Man*. We have already seen that Jesus is often talking about the glorious Son of Man in the prophecy of Daniel. For Jesus this glory begins at the cross (see 23-24). But he knows that it involves all kinds of people (see 32) acknowledging him:

> *In my vision at night I looked, and there before me was one like a son of man, coming with the clouds of heaven. He approached the Ancient of Days and was led into his presence. He was given authority, glory and sovereign power; all nations and peoples of every language worshipped him.*
>
> (Daniel 7:13-14a)

3. – The crowd (34-36)

People listening have questions about the expression *lifted up* and about who Jesus means when he is talking about the Son of Man (see 34).

Rather than answer the questions, Jesus tells the crowd that they need to make a decision. There is a battle taking place between light and darkness; so, he says, *walk while you have the light, before darkness overtakes you* (35b).

And Jesus explains what he means: *Believe in the light while you have the light, so that you may become children of light* (36a).

He will return to this invitation before Section Five is over.

Block Y. The rejection (12:37-43)

1. – The surprise (37)

John tells it like it is: *Even after Jesus had performed so many signs in their presence, they still would not believe in him.* This has been a theme throughout the Gospel: while many became curious about Jesus because of his signs, others seem dead set against really believing in him (see, for example, chapter 2:23-25; 4:48).

This is astonishing. When you consider the signs we have seen, it seems extraordinary that anyone would refuse to believe in Jesus.

So John tells us why this happens.

2. – The explanation (38-41)

The prophet Isaiah gives us the reasons for a refusal to believe.

First, Isaiah tells us that this is a common phenomenon. Talking about the coming of the suffering servant of the Lord, he asks: *Lord, who has believed our message, and to whom has the arm of the Lord been revealed?* (38, quoting Isa 53:1)

It's worth noticing that Isaiah calls the servant *the arm of the Lord.* If Jesus is the servant (see Isaiah chapter 42:1-4; 49:6), that is saying something about who Jesus is. My arm is *part of me*; by calling Jesus *the arm of the Lord* Isaiah is saying that he is God himself.

And second, Isaiah tells us that it is part of God's purpose that some will refuse to believe: *He has blinded their eyes and hardened their hearts, so they can neither see with their eyes, nor understand with their hearts, nor turn – and I would heal them* (40, quoting Isa 6:10).

Isaiah received this message when he saw the glory of God in the temple (see Isa chapter 6:3). God *prevents* people responding in a superficial way, or, as Jesus himself says, *No one can come to me unless the Father who sent me draws them* (see chapter 6:44a).

There is one last thing here. Do you remember, says John, when Isaiah saw the glory of God in the temple? Actually *he saw Jesus' glory and spoke about him* (41b).

People who look at Jesus are looking at God.

3. – The reaction (42-43)

Despite the widespread unbelief, *many even among the leaders believed in him* (42a).

But John tells us that they refused to announce this to others because they were afraid of excommunication from the synagogue and so from the community (see 42b).

And the reason for that is that *they loved human praise more than praise from God* (43).

Which is a warning for us all.

Block Z. The invitation (12:44-50)

These are the last words of Jesus to the crowds before he goes to the cross. And he wants to get his message out. As John says, *Jesus cried out...* (44a).

1. – The necessity of faith (44-46)

Jesus spells it out: *The one who looks at me is seeing the one who sent me* (45). He is claiming to be God.

And whoever believes in him is also believing in the Father (see 44), and will no longer be stumbling around in darkness but will know Jesus as the light (see 46).

These wonderful promises are an invitation to believe in Jesus.

2. – The certainty of judgment (47-48)

Jesus makes it very clear why he has come: *I did not come to judge the world, but to save the world* (47b).

But there will be judgment and there will be a Judgment Day. And for those who have rejected Jesus, *the very words I have spoken will condemn them at the last day* (48b).

These solemn words should make us ask ourselves how *we* are responding to Jesus' words.

3. – The message of the Son (49-50)

Jesus gives such extraordinary weight to his own words because *the Father who sent me commanded me to say all that I have spoken* (49b); *whatever I say is just what the Father has told me to say* (50b).

And here is the good news: *I know that his command leads to eternal life* (50a).

Jesus offers eternal life to all those who accept his words. This is the invitation once again: Jesus calls us to believe in him and so experience life (see chapter 20:30-31).

Learning the Gospel

Although Section Five is so full of content it is easy to learn the outline. Again, start with the headings in bold.

The second stage is to add the sub-headings. If you are not happy about my sub-headings I have no problem if you replace them with your own. I will never know!

The basic structure of Section Five can be learnt by most people in ten minutes.

Section Five: The Judgment

Two signs

A. The anointing in Bethany

    1. What Mary does
    2. How Judas reacts
    3. What Jesus says

B. The arrival in Jerusalem

    1. The arrival
    2. The meaning
    3. The reaction

Three blocks

X. The decision

    1. Jesus
    2. The Father
    3. The crowd

Y. The rejection

    1. The surprise

2. The explanation
3. The reaction

Z. The invitation

1. The necessity of faith
2. The certainty of judgment
3. The message of the Son

Meeting the Lord

Although Section Five consists of only one chapter, the content is really important.

Once again, as you tell yourself the two signs, or meet up with a friend to do this together, fill in as many details as you can remember, and talk to the Lord at the same time. Tell him you want your love for him to grow and that you want to express your love to him, as Mary did hers. And acknowledge that he is the Messiah-King.

Now do the same thing with the three blocks. You won't get all the details, but you will find yourself responding to Jesus. Thank him for his willingness to die to give life to others; thank him for his invitation to believe in him and so receive life.

And as *you* are growing in your understanding of Jesus in John's Gospel, *he* is growing in your life and personality. You are meeting the Lord.

Section Six: The Love (John 13:1 - 20:31)
First half: John 13:1 - 17:26

The stage has been set. As Jesus has been teaching the crowds the opposition from the religious authorities has been growing. Now, as he faces the trauma of his crucifixion, Jesus takes time to prepare his disciples for all that is to come. In chapters 1-12 of John's Gospel the word *love* occurs nine times, while in chapters 13-17 we will see it thirty times: here in Section Six we will witness the greatest act of love the world has ever seen.

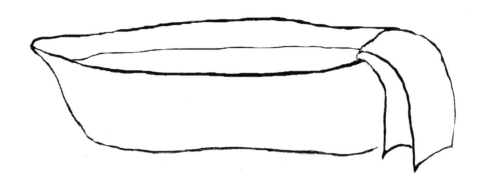

He poured water into a basin
and began to wash his disciples' feet,
drying them with the towel
that was wrapped round him.

John 13:5

Enjoying the View

Three blocks

X. Jesus and his friends (13:1 - 16:33)

1. The last supper (13:1-38)

   a. Jesus: his love (1-5)
   b. Peter: his objection (6-11)
   c. Disciples: our task (12-17)
   b'. Judas: his betrayal (18-30)
   a'. Jesus: his command to love (31-35)

2. The last teaching (14:1 - 16:33)

   a. Jesus: he's leaving (14:1-14)
     i.   He is the way (1-5)
     ii. He is the truth (7-11)
     iii. He is the life (12-14)
   b. The Spirit: he's coming (14:15-31)
     i.   Love for the soul (18-24)
     ii. Truth for the world (25-26)
     iii. Peace for the heart (27-31)
   c. Disciples: our priorities (15:1 - 16:3)
     i.   The relationship to Jesus (1-11)
     ii. The relationship to one another (12-17)
     iii. The relationship to the world (15:18 - 16:3)
   b'. The Spirit: he's coming (16:4-15)
     i.   He brings the presence of Jesus (4-7)
     ii. He spreads the message of Jesus (8-11)
     iii. He completes the revelation of Jesus (12-15)
   a'. Jesus: he's leaving (16:16-33)
     i.   He promises them joy (19-24)
     ii. He reminds them of love (25-28)
     iii. He offers them peace (29-33)

Y. Jesus and his Father (17:1-26)

   1. Jesus prays for himself (1-5)
   2. Jesus prays for the apostles (6-19)
   3. Jesus prays for us (20-26)

Z. Jesus and his enemies (18:1 - 19:16)

Two signs
A. The crucifixion (19:17-42)
B. The resurrection (20:1-29)

One purpose

(We will focus on Part Z and on the two signs when we consider the second half of Section Six – see page 109ff.)

John begins Section Six by telling us two vital facts. First, the events we are about to read about happened just before the Jewish Passover Festival, which will help us to understand the *meaning* of the death and resurrection of Jesus. And, second, we learn the *motive* for what Jesus is about to do: *Having loved his own who were in the world, he loved them to the end* (chapter 13:1).

It is natural to assume that the footwashing at the beginning of chapter 13 is one of the signs in this section. But I think it makes much more sense to say that the two signs are at the *end* of the section because they are the climax of the Gospel: Jesus dies on the cross and rises again.

So what is the relationship between the footwashing and the events of the cross and the resurrection?

It seems to me that the footwashing, while of course being a historical account of something that happened at the last supper, is also an *acted parable* of Jesus and his work. John says as much: Jesus washed the disciples' feet because he knew *that he had come from God and was returning to God* (chapter 13:3-4).

So Jesus *got up from the meal* (4a), just as he had got up from his throne in heaven; he *took off his outer clothing* (4), just as he had laid aside his glory. Then Jesus *wrapped a towel around his waist* (4b), just as he had come into the world as a servant. And then he *began to wash his disciples' feet* (5), just as he went to the cross to wash our sins away (see also 8,10).

After all this, Jesus *put on his clothes and returned to his place* (12b), just as he returned to glory and sat down at his Father's right hand.

So the footwashing points us to the whole work of Jesus and especially to the two signs of his cross and resurrection at the end of Section Six (see Philippians 2:5-11 for a similar down-and-up description of what Jesus has done).

The three blocks in this section are the lead-up to the dying and rising of Jesus, and tell us about Jesus and his friends, Jesus and his Father, and Jesus and his enemies.

In Block X Jesus is getting his disciples ready for what is to come; in Block Y he is praying to his Father as he faces the cross; and in Block Z he is arrested, accused and condemned by his enemies.

Before reading further it would be good to read the account as John gives it to us in his Gospel. Start at chapter 13:1 and read through to the end of chapter 17. Try to imagine every scene as you read, and to imagine the emotions of those involved, too.

There is power in the word of God!

Unpacking the Content

Three blocks

Block X. Jesus and his friends (13:1 - 16:33)

1. – The last supper (13:1-38)

With chapter 13 we are at the last supper: this is the last time Jesus eats with his disciples before he goes to the cross. John doesn't tell us about the sharing of the bread and wine and their meaning, perhaps because he knows that Mark has already done that in his Gospel (see Mark 14:22-26).

What John *does* do is show us Jesus preparing his friends for what is to come.

The passage is written with mirror links, which makes it easier to commit it to memory.

a. – Jesus: his love (1-5)

John makes it very clear that Jesus knows three things. First, he knows that it is time to go to the cross (see 1b); second, he knows that *the Father had put all things under his power* (3a); and, third, he knows *that he had come from God and was returning to God* (3b). And he certainly knows that Judas is going to betray him (see 2, also verse 11 and Mark 14:18).

So Jesus is completely aware of his Father's plan and of his own authority.

Now comes the shock. John does not tell us that Jesus washed his disciples' feet *despite* his knowledge and authority, but *because* of it: so he *got up from the meal* (4).

You can imagine all conversation drying up as Jesus prepares to do a slave's work. When Jesus *began to wash his disciples' feet*, we know that this is an act of love (see 1b).

b. – Peter: his objection (6-11)

Doubtless Peter is simply putting into words what the other disciples have been thinking: *Lord, are you going to wash my feet?* (6b) But then he turns his question into a prohibition: *You shall never wash my feet* (8).

When Jesus corrects him, Peter decides he wants his whole body to be washed (see 8b-9). So now Jesus explains something of vital importance.

Peter and most of his friends *are clean* (10b), which means that they are forgiven because they have believed the words Jesus has spoken to them (see chapter 5:24 and chapter 15:3). So there is no need for the bath Peter wants.

Only Judas has not been washed, because only Judas has refused to believe in Jesus (see 11).

c. – Disciples: our task (12-17)

After Jesus has got dressed again and sat down, he explains the significance of what he has just done: *Now that I, your Lord and Teacher, have washed your feet, you also should wash one another's feet* (14).

The lesson is clear. If Jesus was willing to be a servant to his friends, they should bc willing to be servants to each other.

This is staggering teaching, which Jesus underlines by telling his disciples that he has given them *an example that you should do as I have done for you* (15).

Humble service is part of a disciple's task, and it brings a reward with it: *Now that you know these things, you will be blessed if you do them* (17). The deliberate decision to turn Jesus' love into practical action is one none of us will ever regret.

b'. – Judas: his betrayal (18-30)

Jesus is very clear that he is going to be betrayed by one of his own friends and that this will be a fulfilment of Old Testament Scripture (see 18-20).

But the very thought shakes Jesus to the core of his being: he is *troubled in spirit* (21). The expression speaks of revulsion and agitation.

The disciples, understandably, want to know what Jesus is getting at. So Peter speaks to *the disciple whom Jesus loved* (23), urging him to ask Jesus who the betrayer is going to be.

The disciple whom Jesus loved is almost certainly John the Gospel-writer (see the larger commentaries for the evidence). John never refers to himself by name, but he does use this expression a number of times in Section Six (see also chapter 19:26; 20:2; 21:7,20). The most natural conclusion is that John is talking about himself.

This does not have to mean that Jesus loved John *more* than he loved the other disciples. It could just be that John never stopped being surprised that Jesus loved *him*.

So John asks his question and Jesus, using a sign, points the finger at Judas (see 25-27). It's possible that only John and Peter have a glimmer of understanding as to what is happening here.

The mirror link with part b (see 6-11) contrasts Peter with Judas. They both get things wrong. But while Peter is willing to learn from his Master, Judas is determined to go through with his plan to betray Jesus.

After Judas has left, John adds that *it was night* (30). It certainly was night, but John is almost certainly telling us that it was night in Judas' heart, too.

a'. – Jesus: his command to love (31-35)

Jesus knows that the time has come to go to the cross: he tells his disciples that *now the Son of Man is glorified and God is glorified in him* (31).

But how are the followers of Jesus to live after he has left them (see 33)? They receive a new command from their Master to help them answer this question: *As I have loved you, so you must love one another* (34b).

The phrase *as I have loved you* adds extraordinary power to the command: Jesus' self-giving love, pouring himself out for them, is to be the model for their own love to each other. And the mirror link to part a (see 1-5) gives us an example of that love in action.

And love like this will make it clear to others that the disciples are the real thing (see 35). Most people need to *see* the gospel before they can *hear and understand* it: love within the Jesus community is for many visible evidence that these are genuine followers of Jesus.

At the end of chapter 13 there is a crucial bridge into the next part of Jesus' interaction with his disciples.

Peter's comment to Jesus that *I will lay down my life for you* (37b) is stupid, but of course he says it because he loves Jesus.

We are not told how the disciples reacted to Jesus' response to Peter. He looks at his friend and tells him that *before the cock crows, you will disown me three times!* (38b)

The stage is set for what is to come.

2. – The last teaching (14:1 - 16:33)

In chapters 14, 15 and 16 Jesus is still saying goodbye to his disciples and preparing them for life without his being physically present with them. Some of it they won't understand until after his death and resurrection.

It looks like chapter 14 happens in the Upper Room where the last supper has taken place. Jesus probably says the words of chapters 15 and 16 as he and his disciples are on the way to the Garden of Gethsemane (see the last sentence of chapter 14).

Because of Jesus' love we can be sure that his last teaching to the disciples before he goes to the cross is of vital importance for them. We need to hear it too.

The mirror linking in these three chapters will help us to understand Jesus' teaching, as well as to commit it to memory.

a. – Jesus: he's leaving (14:1-14)

This will be a shock for the disciples: this news is here in these verses (see 2-4,12) and is repeated in the next two chapters (see especially part a', chapter 16:16-33).

It will help the disciples to cope with his departure if they remember who Jesus is: his key statement here is *I am the way and the truth and the life* (6a). Rather than *pointing* to the way, the truth and the life Jesus *embodies* these things, and so is unique: *No one comes to the Father except through me* (6b).

Verse 6 is like the *Contents* page for this passage. Jesus is explaining what he means.

i. – He is the way (1-5)

Jesus is going to his Father's house (see 2), which is an image for what we might call *heaven*. And he is very clear: *I am going there to prepare a place for you* (2b).

So Jesus is the way for us to get to heaven. His promise *I will come back and take you to be with me* (3) may be a reference to his second coming in glory as well as to what he does for every disciple when they die: he collects us and takes us to heaven.

Only Jesus can do this (see 6b). And from our side of the cross we know why: only Jesus has died for our sins and so, in his love, earned us the forgiveness that puts us right with God.

ii. – He is the truth (7-11)

Talking about his Father, Jesus tells his disciples that they *have seen him* (7b). And now, in answer to a request from Philip, Jesus spells out what he means: *Anyone who has seen me has seen the Father* (9b).

It is an extraordinary claim. If you want to know the truth about God, says Jesus, look at me. He has already made such claims (see, for example, chapter 5:18, 8:58 and 10:30); but now, once again, Jesus is unmistakeably claiming to be God.

He reinforces this by adding *I am in the Father and the Father is in me* (11a). Jesus, the eternal Son of God, is in an intimate relationship with his Father, which more than justifies his claim to *be* the truth.

iii. – He is the life (12-14)

Real life is knowing Jesus and living in relationship with him. But what does Jesus mean when he says that believers will do *greater things* than his own miracles (see 12)?

One possible answer comes with realising that someone coming to faith in Jesus is a greater miracle than 5,000 people being fed with one boy's packed lunch. It may be that Jesus is saying that all who follow him will help others to trust him for themselves.

And they will be able to do this *because I am going to the Father* (12b). This is a reference to the coming of the Spirit, who could not come until Jesus had returned to his Father (see chapter 7:39) and who would bring people to faith (see chapter 16:7-8).

Real life, says Jesus, means seeing God the Father answering the requests we bring him *in my name* (13). This is not a magic formula, but a recognition that we can only have access to God because of who Jesus is and what, in his love, he has done for us.

And Jesus even tells his disciples that they *may ask me for anything in my name* (14a). We can bring prayers to Jesus as well as to God the Father.

So begins the last teaching of Jesus to his disciples before he goes to the cross. He is going away, but they are to remember – and they will experience it, too – that he is the way, the truth and the life.

b. – The Spirit: he's coming (14:15-31)

This is the second piece of news Jesus tells his friends in chapter 14 of John's Gospel. And the logic is simple: if Jesus is no longer going to be physically present with the disciples, how are they to continue to follow him?

The answer is that the Holy Spirit will be with them.

At this stage Jesus calls him *the Spirit of truth* (17a) and describes him as an *advocate* (the word also means *comforter* and *encourager*) (16).

And then Jesus tells his disciples that the Spirit *lives with you and will be in you* (17b). In other words, they could already reckon with the Spirit's *presence*, but would soon begin to experience his *living inside them*.

This is New Covenant language. As we have already seen, there were Old Testament promises that, with the coming of the New Covenant, believers would have the Holy Spirit living within them (see my comments on chapter 7:37-39; also Ezek 36:25-27 and Joel 2:28-32).

It is these promises which Jesus will make reality. And, because he loves his disciples and in order to whet their appetite, he tells them what his gift of the Spirit will provide (see also part b', chapter 16:4-15).

i. – Love for the soul (18-24)

Jesus tells his friends that the Spirit in them will mean that Jesus is present: *I will not leave you as orphans; I will come to you* (18).

The disciples can show their love for him by obeying his commands (see 21a and 15). But then Jesus says something extraordinary: *The one who loves me will be loved by my Father* (21b).

Does this mean that God starts to love us when we start obeying his commands? Surely not: the Bible is very clear that God loved us before we ever started to think of him (see, for example, 1 John 4:19).

No, it must be that Jesus is talking here about the disciples *experiencing* God's love. He is promising that anyone who loves and obeys him will not just *know about* God's love in their heads, but *know it and feel it* in their experience.

He says it again: *Anyone who loves me will obey my teaching. My Father will love them, and we will come to them and make our home with them* (23).

The Spirit brings love for the soul.

ii. – Truth for the world (25-26)

Now Jesus promises that *the Holy Spirit, whom the Father will send in my name, will teach you all things and will remind you of everything I have said to you* (26).

This is not a promise for us who are reading John's Gospel, because we have never heard Jesus' voice speaking to us; the Spirit cannot remind *us* of things Jesus has said to us.

But the apostles have heard so much teaching from Jesus that, left to their own devices, they would be bound to forget some parts and distort others. So Jesus makes this astonishingly generous promise: the Spirit *will remind you of everything I have said to you* (26).

Everything.

This should make us catch our breath again. Jesus is promising that when an apostle passes on his teaching to the world – by writing a Gospel, for example – he will make not a single mistake. Because of the Spirit's work in the disciples, what they write will not be *more or less correct*: it will be *infallibly reliable*.

Jesus is laying the foundation here for the writing of the New Testament. He will return to the subject in chapter 16:13-15.

The Holy Spirit has provided truth for the world.

iii. – Peace for the heart (27-31)

Jesus began chapter 14 by telling his disciples *Do not let your hearts be troubled* (1); now he returns to the same theme (see 27b).

The reason this is important is that Satan (*the prince of this world*) is coming to do his work (see 30). And this will happen as Jesus is submitting to his Father by going to the cross (see 31): indeed, he goes so far as to say that *the Father is greater than I* (28b).

This does not imply that Jesus is less than God.

Yes, the Father sent him into the world (see, for example, chapter 5:24,36-38; 6:38-39,44,57), and Jesus submits to his Father (see, for example, chapter 5:30; 8:29; 10:18b; 12:49-50).

But at the same time Jesus is fully God (see, for example, chapter 1:1,18; 5:18; 8:58; 10:30-33; 14:9; 20:28).

Both of these things are true.

What the disciples need as they face the trauma of the death of their Master and the opposition of the world is *peace*. And this, in the context of the coming of the Holy Spirit, is what Jesus promises them: *Peace I leave with you; my peace I give you* (27a).

Through the Spirit Jesus gives peace for the heart.

c. – Disciples: our priorities (15:1 - 16:3)

It looks like Jesus and the disciples have left the room where their last supper together took place (see chapter 14:31b) and are on their way to the garden where Jesus will be arrested.

We don't know how much the disciples really understood of what they have heard in the Upper Room. But Jesus is still preparing them for the time when he will no longer be physically with them. So now his teaching focuses on what their priorities should be.

So it is obvious what comes first.

i. – The relationship to Jesus (1-11)

In the Old Testament the nation of Israel is sometimes described as a vine, but one which produced only bad grapes (see, for example, Isa 5:1-8).

But now Jesus says *I am the true vine* (1a): he is the fulfilment of all that Israel should have been. He tells his disciples that *you are already clean because of the word I have spoken to you* (3) – in other words, they are already in relationship with him. As he says himself: *I am the vine; you are the branches* (5a).

But this relationship needs to be maintained, so Jesus emphasizes that the disciples (the branches) need to *remain* in Jesus (the vine).

If they don't, it will show that they have never really been in relationship with Jesus at all: *God the Father cuts off every branch in me that bears no fruit* (2a); *if you do not remain in me, you are like a branch that is thrown away and withers* (6a; see also chapter 6:70-71).

But if they do remain in Jesus, they will live fruitful lives, loving him and obeying him (see 9-10). If we maintain this relationship with Jesus, we will *bear fruit* (see 4,5), which also means that our prayers will be answered (see 7; see also chapter 14:13-14).

This fruitbearing doesn't make us into disciples; rather it proves that we *are* disciples of Jesus: *This is to my Father's glory, that you bear much fruit, showing yourselves to be my disciples* (8).

Anyone who claims to be a *follower* of Jesus will make their priority their *relationship* to Jesus.

ii. – The relationship to one another (12-17)

Jesus has already told the disciples about the importance of loving each other (see chapter 13:34). Now he stresses it again: *Love each other as I have loved you* (12); *this is my command: love each other* (17).

That phrase *as I have loved you* (12) should make us think. Jesus explains what love looks like: *Greater love has no one than this: to lay down one's life for one's friends* (13).

Jesus has already talked about the good shepherd laying down his life (see chapter 10:11). Once again he is alluding to the cross, where he will die so that we can be forgiven and set free. This is the greatest sacrifice and the greatest love.

And this, says Jesus, is to be a model for the disciples' relationships with one another. Love means not standing on our rights but instead committing to humble service of others, whatever it costs (see chapter 13:3-15).

Love like this is to be the outstanding characteristic of the community of Jesus followers.

iii. – The relationship to the world (15:18 - 16:3)

The first two relationships were about love; this third one is about the opposite.

Jesus teaches his disciples here that they no longer belong to the world system which hates Jesus (see 18-19): *That is why the world hates you* (19b).

So as they tell others about Jesus they will meet with hostility. As they do so, they will find it helpful to remember that people in the world are also hostile to Jesus and to his Father (see 20-21), an attitude which makes them guilty (22-24).

And this, says Jesus, is hardly a surprise: *This is to fulfil what is written in their Law: 'They hated me without reason'* (25).

This raises a question: how are Jesus' disciples to cope in the context of the world's hostility? The answer is that they have two things which will help them.

First, they have the Spirit of Jesus: *When the Advocate comes, whom I will send to you from the Father – the Spirit of truth who goes out from the Father – he will testify about me* (26). As the disciples tell the world about Jesus, as they must (see 27), the Holy Spirit will be equipping them so they can share their message.

And second, they have the word of Jesus (see chapter 16:1-3). He has told them about the opposition they will encounter *so that you will not fall away* (1b). He has warned them about excommunication from the syna-gogue and the possibility of martyrdom (see 2). Forewarned is forearmed.

And all the while Jesus, in his love, is preparing his friends for the time when he is no longer physically with them. Understanding these three relationships will help the disciples to have clear priorities as they contin-ue to follow him.

But there is more to come.

b'. – The Spirit: he's coming (16:4-15)

Here Jesus is returning to something he spoke to the disciples about while they were still in the Upper Room (see part b, chapter 14:15-31). It will be a massive encouragement to them to hear what the coming Holy Spirit is going to do.

i. – He brings the presence of Jesus (4-7)

Jesus knows that his friends are *filled with grief* (6) because he has told them that he is going away. But the statement *I am going to him who sent me* (5a) should remind them (and us) that his return to the Father will make possible the coming of the Holy Spirit (see my comments on chap-ter 7:37-39).

Jesus tells his disciples that *it is for your good that I am going away* (7a). He explains why: *Unless I go away, the Advocate will not come to you* (7b). So here is the question: why is it better for the disciples to have the Holy Spirit than to have Jesus?

The reason is simple but profound.

Jesus, having taken on humanity (see chapter 1:14a), can only be in one place at a time because he has a human body. So if Jesus were still living physically here on our planet, most believers would not be able to experience his presence.

But the Holy Spirit has no such limitations: he brings the presence of Jesus to every believer wherever they are. That is great news.

ii. – He spreads the message of Jesus (8-11)

When the Holy Spirit comes, says Jesus, *he will prove the world to be in the wrong* (8) about three things. In other words, when the disciples spread the message of Jesus, the Holy Spirit will be spreading it too.

First, he will prove the world wrong *about sin* (9a). Jesus has warned his listeners so often about the seriousness of sin (see, for example, chapter 8:24), but they still *do not believe in me* (9b). And yet the Father's will was that that they *believe in the one he has sent* (chapter 6:29). Rejecting Jesus is sin, and the Holy Spirit will convince people of that.

Second, the Spirit will prove the world wrong *about righteousness* (10a). Some of the religious leaders in Israel had concluded that Jesus was a sinner (see chapter 9:24), thus showing that their idea of righteousness was twisted. And yet we know that Jesus is righteous because he is soon to be exalted: *I am going to the Father* (10).

And third, the Holy Spirit will prove the world wrong *about judgment* (11a). Back in Section Three Jesus had pleaded with the crowd to *stop judging by mere appearances, but instead judge correctly* (see chapter 7:24). Their judgments about Jesus will be shown to be wrong as Satan is defeated by the cross and the empty tomb: *the prince of this world now stands condemned* (11).

This is a huge encouragement for all Christian disciples: the Holy Spirit spreads the message of Jesus.

iii. – He completes the revelation of Jesus (12-15)

Jesus cannot tell his disciples everything they need to hear: *I have much more to say to you, more than you can now bear* (12). But the Holy Spirit will guide the apostles *into all the truth* (13).

Two things are worth pointing out about verse 13. First, with the expression *he, the Spirit* John is bending over backwards to make it clear that the Holy Spirit is not an impersonal power: he is personal and active. And second, he will guide the apostles not into *some of the truth*, but into *all the truth*.

This is an astonishing statement, which could remind us of something Jesus promised in the Upper Room (see my comments on part b, chapter 14:26). By completing the revelation of Jesus, the Spirit *will glorify me because it is from me that he will receive what he will make known to you* (14).

Imagine an actor alone on the stage. Everything is in darkness apart from a huge spotlight pointing to him: the aim of the technician operating the spotlight is to focus everyone's attention on the actor.

The Holy Spirit is like that technician. He *glorifies* Jesus by helping men and women to see Jesus more clearly: he completes the revelation of Jesus.

But now we can put that in the past tense. The revelation of Jesus has already been completed, by the Spirit inspiring the writers of the New Testament (see 1 Cor 2:12-13; 2 Tim 3:16).

And he still brings glory to Jesus as he opens our minds and hearts to understand and receive the message of the Bible.

a'. – Jesus: he's leaving (16:16-33)

In the Upper Room Jesus had given the disciples the disturbing news that he was going to leave them (see part a, chapter 14:1-4,12). Now he returns to the theme: *In a little while you will see me no more* (16a).

Even though Jesus tells them that they will see him again (see 16b), the disciples are confused and sad at the news of Jesus' departure: they *don't understand what he is saying* (18b, and see 17-18).

So Jesus tells his friends what he is going to do for them. These are his last words to them before he goes to the cross.

i. – He promises them joy (19-24)

Jesus is very clear that things are not going to be easy: *You will weep and mourn while the world rejoices* (20a). His arrest, trials and crucifixion will please some, but they will cause his friends heart-breaking sorrow.

But things will not stay like that. Using the image of a woman's pain in childbirth being replaced by joy (see 21), Jesus tells the disciples that *your grief will turn to joy* (20b): *I will see you again and you will rejoice* (22).

They probably do not understand what he is getting at. But from our perspective we can see that Jesus is talking about his resurrection. No wonder he assures them that *no one will take away your joy* (22b).

This new situation will mean a new joy in prayer. Instead of asking Jesus for things the disciples will ask the Father *in my name* (23): as they pray trusting in Jesus and for his glory, they will have direct access to God the Father. And he *will give you whatever you ask in my name* (23).

Jesus knows that this will be a new experience for his friends: *Until now you have not asked for anything in my name* (24a). So he encourages them to do it: *Ask and you will receive, and your joy will be complete* (24b).

ii. – He reminds them of love (25-28)

Jesus reassures the disciples: what he is telling them will become ever clearer (see 25).

And now he says something which must have been a huge comfort to them: *The Father himself loves you* (27a). Jesus has already said that *the Father loves the Son* (see chapter 5:20a), but now he tells his friends that the Father loves them, too.

And he tells them why. The reason is the way that they have responded to him: *The Father himself loves you because you have loved me and have believed that I came from God* (27).

The greatest thing a human being can ever know is that they are loved by God.

iii. – He offers them peace (29-33)

Now the disciples are beginning to understand Jesus better (see 29-30). But he warns them about what is to come: *A time is coming and in fact has come when you will be scattered, each to your own home. You will leave me all alone* (32a).

But with the warning comes a promise. He has told them about all this *so that in me you may have peace* (33a). When the darkness arrives, the certainty that God is in control will fill the disciples with reassurance.

And now Jesus repeats the warning-promise combination. First the warning: *In this world you will have trouble* (33b).

And then the promise: *But take heart! I have overcome the world* (33b). Any follower of Jesus who takes these words to heart will not fail to experience the peace of God.

As we have looked at *Part X: Jesus and his friends* in chapters 13, 14, 15 and 16 of John's Gospel, we have seen him preparing the disciples for life without him being physically present.

Jesus has told them that their relationship with him will continue, that they must be careful to love and serve each other, and that they must reckon with the world's hostility as they continue to follow him.

And he has promised to send them the astonishing gift of the Holy Spirit.

If we are believers in Jesus, all this is for us, too.

Block Y. Jesus and his Father (17:1-26)

This is holy ground. As we listen to the Son of God speaking to his Father, we are getting insight into the most important relationship in the universe.

And, because Jesus is about to go to the cross, we will discover his greatest concerns. There is nothing more important to Jesus than what he prays for here.

So let's listen to God talking to God.

1. – Jesus prays for himself (1-5)

Jesus knows who he is: he is the Son of God (see 1) and the promised Messiah (see 3: *Christ*). And he can talk to his Father of *the glory I had with you before the world began* (5b).

And Jesus knows too that he is about to go to his death: *Father, the hour has come* (1, cf. chapter 2:4; 7:30; 8:20; 12:23,27; 13:1).

What does he pray? *Father, glorify your Son* (1, see also 5a). That would be a weird, self-obsessed prayer if an imperfect person prayed it, but Jesus is the sinless, eternal Son of God. So this prayer is absolutely right.

And he prays that the Father will glorify him, so *that your Son may glorify you* (1). The glory of God is a technical term for the *god-ness* of God: the glory of God is what makes God God.

So Jesus wants people to see the glory of God, both in his Father and in him. He wants people to admire God, to honour God and to worship God.

2. – Jesus prays for the apostles (6-19)

Some of what Jesus prays here can be applied to us, too; but the focus is on the apostles.

Jesus begins by *describing* them. The Father had *given* them to Jesus (see 6,7,9) and Jesus has *revealed* the Father to them (see 6). They have *accepted* and *obeyed* his teaching (see 8a, 6b), *believed* that the Father has sent him (see 8b), and so have brought him *glory* (see 10b).

We can sense how precious the apostles are to Jesus. And now he prays two things for them.

First, he prays for their protection. Jesus has protected the disciples while he has been with them (see 12a); but now *Holy Father, protect them by the power of your name* (11).

They need to be protected from disunity, *so that they may be one as we are one* (11b). But they also need protection from Satan in the context of the world's hostility to their message: *My prayer is not that you take them out of the world, but that you protect them from the evil one* (15).

So, *second*, Jesus prays for their growth in holiness: *Sanctify them by the truth; your word is truth* (17). He has sent the disciples *into* the world (see 18b), but they are not *of* the world (see 14b), so they need to be growing more and more like their Master.

And Jesus knows that this will become reality as the truth (the word of God, see 17) does its work in their lives. Of course the Holy Spirit uses other things; but what he will use more than anything else to make the apostles holy is the word of God. And that is what Jesus prays for them.

3. – Jesus prays for us (20-26)

But Jesus is not only thinking of the apostles: *My prayer is not for them alone. I pray also for those who will believe in me through their message* (20). Once again, he asks his Father for two things.

First, he prays for their unity, *that all of them may be one* (21a). And Jesus shows us the kind of unity he is thinking of by comparing it with the unity between him and his Father: he is praying *that they may be one as we are one* (22b).

This is obviously so important that Jesus says it again: the goal is *I in them and you in me – so that they may be brought to complete unity* (23a).

And what will happen if Jesus' followers relate to one another in a unity which reflects the unity between the Father and the Son? The answer is clear: *the world will know that you sent me and have loved them even as you have loved me* (23b; see also 21b and chapter 13:35).

Second, Jesus prays that all who follow him will one day be with him in eternity: *Father, I want those you have given me to be with me where I am, and to see my glory, the glory you have given me because you loved me before the creation of the world* (24).

The most wonderful thing about what we often call *heaven* is being with Jesus and seeing his glory.

Jesus' prayer reaches its climax as he commits himself to revealing his Father: *I have made you known to them, and will continue to make you known in order that the love you have for me may be in them and that I myself may be in them* (26).

As we listen to Jesus praying to his Father, all of us who follow him realise how much we have to look forward to!

Learning the Gospel

Remember that we are only talking here about learning the order of the events of the first half of Section Six (chapter 13:1 - 17:26).

First, learn the headings in bold. Then, when you have done that, add the sub-headings.

Knowing that a friend is also learning the order of the events will help you to commit yourself to doing it too.

As this half-section is quite long it may take some determination to learn it. But the mirror linking, both in the last supper and in the last teaching of Jesus before he goes to the cross, makes this significantly easier.

And it is so worth it.

Section Six: The Love (first half)

Three blocks

X. Jesus and his friends

1. The last supper

   a. Jesus: his love
   b. Peter: his objection
   c. Disciples: our task
   b'. Judas: his betrayal
   a'. Jesus: his command to love

2. The last teaching

a. Jesus: he's leaving
   i.   He is the way
   ii. He is the truth
   iii. He is the life

b. The Spirit: he's coming
   i.   Love for the soul
   ii. Truth for the world
   iii. Peace for the heart

c. Disciples: our priorities
   i.   The relationship to Jesus
   ii. The relationship to one another
   iii. The relationship to the world

b'. The Spirit: he's coming
   i.   He brings the presence of Jesus
   ii. He spreads the message of Jesus
   iii. He completes the revelation of Jesus

a'. Jesus: he's leaving
   i.   He promises them joy
   ii. He reminds them of love
   iii. He offers them peace

Y. Jesus and his Father

   1. Jesus prays for himself
   2. Jesus prays for the apostles
   3. Jesus prays for us

Meeting the Lord

It is absolutely worthwhile to run through this material in your head, using the sub-headings to remind yourself of some of the details. Or you could meet up with a friend and do this together.

As you remember Jesus talking about his identity and promising to send the Holy Spirit, you may find yourself worshipping. As you think about the three relationships that disciples experience, you may want to pray that you will live as a disciple should. As you remember what the Holy Spirit has come to do, you will find yourself expecting to see him at work more and more.

And as you hear Jesus talking to his Father, you will be wanting to know him better.

You will be meeting the Lord.

Section Six: The Love (John 13:1 - 20:31)
Second half: John 18:1 - 20:31

Jesus has prepared his friends for what is to come by teaching them about his departure and about the coming Holy Spirit, and he has prepared *himself* by praying to his Father. Now he goes out to meet his enemies (see chapter 18:1,4). The events which unfold will lead inexorably to Jesus' suffering and death. But this death is not a defeat: it will be followed by a resurrection.

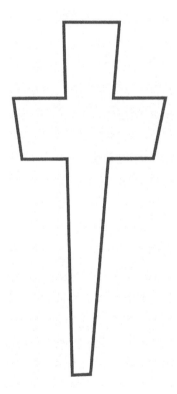

Carrying his own cross,
he went out to the place of the Skull
(which in Aramaic is called Golgatha).
There they crucified him.

John 19:17-18a

Enjoying the View

Three blocks

X. Jesus and his friends (13:1 - 16:33)
Y. Jesus and his Father (17:1-26)

Z. Jesus and his enemies (18:1 - 19:16)

  1. Jesus arrested (18:1-14)
  2. Jesus denied (18:15-27)
  3. Jesus condemned (18:28 - 19:16)

Two signs

A. The crucifixion (19:17-42)

  1. See him crucified (17-27)
  2. Hear him die (28-30)
  3. Respond to his love (31-42)

B. The resurrection (20:1-29)

  1. The tomb was empty (1-10)
  2. Jesus appeared (11-18)
  3. The disciples were transformed (19-29)

One purpose (20:30-31)

Probably the events of this second half of Section Six will be more familiar to most of us than the events of the first half.

It would be good to read through chapter 18:1 - chapter 20:31. As you do so, try to imagine the emotions of all those involved. Ask God to make it live to you: it might be a help for some of us to read it aloud.

And feel free to stop sometimes to worship. This does not need only to be about information: it can also be about encounter.

Unpacking the Content

Three blocks

(We looked at Blocks X and Y earlier: see page 88ff.)

Block Z. Jesus and his enemies (18:1 - 19:16)

After time spent with his friends and time spent with his Father, Jesus is now confronted by his enemies.

The tragedy is that, when faced with their hostility, Jesus is let down by one of his closest friends (see chapter 18:15-18,25-27).

1. – Jesus arrested (18:1-14)

The garden to which Jesus leads his disciples in verse 1 is Gethsemane. It could be that Jesus' prayer asking for the cup of suffering to be taken away from him (which John chooses not to record) happened between verses 1 and 2.

What John *does* tell us is what happens when the mob of soldiers and officials led to the garden by Judas announce that they are looking for *Jesus of Nazareth* (5a). Jesus replies *I am he* (5).

This could be simply Jesus saying *That's me*. But in the Greek, he says *I am*, which, as we have already noted, is the name by which God revealed himself to Moses from the burning bush (see chapter 6:20; 8:58 and Exod 3:14).

What may nudge us in the direction of the view that Jesus is revealing his deity here is the reaction of the mob: John tells us that *they drew back and fell to the ground* (5b).

But Simon Peter resorts to violence. Drawing his sword, he *struck the high priest's servant, cutting off his right ear* (10). Jesus tells Peter to stop fighting, and adds *Shall I not drink the cup the Father has given me?* (11)

So, says John, *they arrested Jesus* (12). They take him first of all not to Caiaphas the high priest, but to Annas, who had been high priest before him and who still has the title and the authority which go with it.

There is a reminder here that *Caiaphas was the one who had advised the Jewish leaders that it would be good if one man died for the people* (14). John wants us to have this in mind as we approach the cross.

2. – Jesus denied (18:15-27)

The other disciple with Peter (see 15) is almost certainly John himself (see the larger commentaries for details).

In the Upper Room Jesus had warned that Peter would deny him (see chapter 13:38). Now the warning is going to become reality.

A servant-girl says to Peter: *You aren't one of this man's disciples too, are you?* (17a) His reply is short and to the point: *I am not* (17b).

Before John tells us about the second and third denials, he tells us about the conversation between Annas and Jesus. This suggests that these things are all going on at the same time.

The effect is powerful: while they are starting to interrogate Jesus with a view to execution, one of his closest friends is denying all knowledge of him.

Jesus gets a slap in the face for asking why there is a need for all this questioning (see 20-22). But he simply asks *If I spoke the truth, why did you strike me?* (23b)

Now John tells us that *Annas sent him bound to Caiaphas the high priest* (24). He does not record this second interrogation, which probably happens while Peter is denying his friend again (see Mark 14:53-72).

Those second and third denials are recounted very briefly. John records the third like this: *Again Peter denied it, and at that moment a cock began to crow* (27).

Peter is behaving as if he had never known Jesus.

3. – Jesus condemned (18:28 - 19:16)

Of course the initial cross-examination of Jesus has already taken place (see chapter 18:19-24). But now *the Jewish leaders took Jesus from Caiaphas to the palace of the Roman governor* (28a).

In these verses Pilate, the Roman governor, interrogates Jesus twice. On each occasion he does this after the religious leaders have put him under pressure to pronounce Jesus guilty. And, after each interrogation, Pilate gives his verdict.

The first interrogation (18:28-40). The Jewish leaders make it plain to Pilate that Jesus is *a criminal*: otherwise *we would not have handed him over to you* (30). And they remind the governor that only he has the legal right to condemn someone to death (see 31).

So Pilate goes into the palace and asks the prisoner if he is *the king of the Jews* (33b). Jesus replies by stating that *my kingdom is not of this world* (36a), and that *the reason I was born and came into the world is to testify to the truth* (37).

Pilate reacts scornfully to Jesus by asking *What is truth?* (38a) But when he goes out to tell the religious leaders his verdict, he says *I find no basis for a charge against him* (38b). He offers to release Jesus, but they want Barabbas, a murderer, instead (see 39-40).

So after this first interrogation, Pilate's verdict is *Not guilty*.

Before the second interrogation begins, John tells us how Pilate and the soldiers humiliate Jesus (see chapter 19:1-3). A crown of thorns and a purple robe make mockery of his kingship (see 2); Pilate has him whipped (see 1); and the soldiers go up to him *again and again, saying, 'Hail, king of the Jews!'* (3)

And Jesus lets it all happen (compare chapter 18:11b).

The second interrogation (19:4-16). Pilate comes out of the palace again and repeats his conclusion that *I find no basis for a charge against him* (4b). But when the religious leaders see Jesus they shout *Crucify! Crucify!* (6a)

When Pilate tells them for the third time that he finds Jesus not guilty (see 6b, also 4b and chapter 18:38), the leaders explain that Jesus *must die, because he claimed to be the Son of God* (7b).

So Pilate goes back into the palace and cross-examines Jesus for a second time. When Jesus refuses to answer his questions, he asks him *Don't you realise I have power either to free you or to crucify you?* (10b)

Jesus' reply is staggering: *You would have no power over me if it were not given to you from above* (11a). This seems to have made Pilate all the more determined that Jesus should not be condemned to death.

But the Jewish leaders are not giving up. They shout something which must have made Pilate uneasy: *If you let this man go, you are no friend of Caesar* (12).

The governor's verdict is still *Not guilty*, but the shouts of *Take him away! Crucify him!* (15a) are too much for him. His own future prospects are more important to him than the truth about Jesus.

So John writes: *Finally Pilate handed him over to them to be crucified* (16b). Jesus has been condemned to death by crucifixion.

Two signs

Sign A. The crucifixion (19:17-42)

1. – See him crucified (17-27)

John wants us to notice three things as Jesus is hanging on the cross.

First, Pilate's notice. Fastened to the wood above Jesus, it reads *Jesus of Nazareth, the King of the Jews* (19b). Pilate has clearly gone to the trouble of having it written *in Aramaic, Latin and Greek* (20b), which means that it could be understood by everyone.

With this, does John want to remind us that Jesus has already been described in his Gospel as *the Saviour of the world* (see chapter 4:42b; see also chapter 1:29)?

When the chief priests demand that the notice should say Jesus *claimed* to be the King of the Jews, Pilate's reply is unyielding: *What I have written, I have written* (22).

Is he still standing by his verdict that Jesus is innocent? We don't know. But what we *do* know is that John is wanting us to recognise Jesus as our king.

Second, Scripture's fulfilment. The soldiers on duty divide up Jesus' clothes between them (see 23a). But because his undergarment is one piece of cloth, without seams, they don't want to tear it but cast lots instead.

John tells us this happened *that the scripture might be fulfilled that said, 'They divided my clothes among them and cast lots for my garment'* (24b, and see Ps 22:18).

The message is clear: the crucifixion of Jesus is part of God's plan. As we see Jesus crucified, naked and humiliated, it may not look like God is in control.

But he is.

And, *third*, Jesus' love. Despite the agony of the cross, Jesus notices his mother, and John too (*the disciple whom he loved*, 26).

He says to his mother *Woman, here is your son*, and to John *Here is your mother* (26b-27a). Jesus' suffering does not result in his turning *away* from others, because he is suffering *for* others: he is showing his love for his mother.

And so, says John, *from that time on, this disciple took her into his home* (27b).

2. – Hear him die (28-30)

Of all the other things Jesus said from the cross, we hear only two.

First, he says *I am thirsty* (28b). This is a way of asking for a drink, of course (see 29). But John tells us two other reasons why Jesus says this.

He says it, *knowing that everything had now been finished* (28a). The job is done. With his death the Saviour of the world has done what he came to do (see also chapter 4:34 and chapter 17:4).

But Jesus says this also so that Scripture will *be fulfilled* (28). This may be a reference to a psalm in which a dying man cries out *My mouth is dried up like a potsherd, and my tongue sticks to the roof of my mouth* (Ps 22:15a).

We are to be under no illusion: everything which happens here is in accordance with the divine plan.

Second, Jesus says *It is finished* (30a). This is not a cry of defeat, but a proclamation of victory. The word was also used in the first century to refer to the payment of a bill, so you could say that Jesus is shouting out *Paid!*

Jesus has paid the price for our sins. He has taken the punishment we deserve. And he has done all this *in his death.*

With that, says John, *he bowed his head and gave up his spirit* (30b).

3. – Respond to his love (31-42)

It is very clear that Jesus has really died. The soldiers come to break the legs of the men on the crosses (see 32), in order to bring much nearer the moment of their death.

But when they come to Jesus they *found that he was already dead* (33). There is no way that they are mistaken: crucifying criminals is part of their job description.

So, instead of breaking his legs, *one of the soldiers pierced Jesus' side with a spear, bringing a sudden flow of blood and water* (34). Whatever the medical explanation (see the larger commentaries for details), this is clear evidence that death has taken place.

And John wants us to know that we are reading an eye-witness account: *The man who saw it has given testimony, and his testimony is true* (35a).

But the death of Jesus is not only a fact of history. John tells us that *these things happened so that the scripture would be fulfilled: 'Not one of his bones will be broken'* (36).

The quotation is from Psalm 34:20, but surely there is also a reference here to the Passover lambs (see Exod 12:46), which died so that the Israelites could escape God's judgment.

The man described by John the Baptist as *the Lamb of God, who takes away the sin of the world* (see chapter 1:29) has died on a cross, as the perfect fulfilment of the Passover lambs. Jesus has died as a substitute for sinners, so that we can be forgiven.

John wants us to respond to this astonishing love. So he tells us about Joseph of Arimathea, a secret follower of Jesus, who now gets Pilate's permission to take the body of Jesus (see 38).

But he has some help. Nicodemus, a member of the Jewish Council and one of the leading teachers in Israel (see chapter 3:1,10), comes with Joseph. They prepare the body for burial and lay Jesus in a tomb near at hand (see 40-42).

Joseph had *feared the Jewish leaders* (38b), as Nicodemus will have, too. But now they can no longer stand at a distance, so we see them outing themselves as Jesus disciples.

They are responding to Jesus' love.

John wants us, his readers, to do the same. He has already told us that he has recorded these things *so that you also may believe* (35b). But now he is encouraging us to imitate Joseph and Nicodemus, by openly declaring that we are followers of Jesus.

This may be a good moment for all of us to thank Jesus for his love in dying for our sins.

Sign B. The resurrection (20:1-29)

If Jesus had stayed dead, we would have no way of knowing if his cry of *It is finished* was true or not. In raising Jesus to life God the Father is telling us that the price really has been paid.

But how do we know that this really happened? John tells us about a historical event, but in addition to that he wants us to know the *evidence* for the resurrection of Jesus.

He majors on three aspects.

1. – The tomb was empty (1-10)

When Mary Magdalene discovers that the stone has been rolled away from the entrance to the tomb, John doesn't mention that she looks inside (see 1).

But she must have: she runs to two of the disciples to tell them that *they have taken the Lord out of the tomb, and we don't know where they have put him!* (2b)

The two disciples are Simon Peter and John (though once again he is not named but is *the one Jesus loved*). Immediately they start out for the tomb, but with no expectation of good news: *they still did not understand from Scripture that Jesus had to rise from the dead* (9).

John, being younger, gets there first. We can imagine him gasping for breath as he *looked in at the strips of linen lying there* (5). But he *did not go in* (5b).

I'm sure that as John is writing this his memory is crystal clear. He remembers that *Simon Peter came along behind him and went straight into the tomb* (6).

Peter sees *the strips of linen lying there, as well as the cloth that had been wrapped round Jesus' head* (6b-7a). *The cloth,* says John, *was still lying in its place, separate from the linen* (7b).

But there is no mention of Peter seeing the body of Jesus. And the linen strips and the head cloth are evidence. Jesus had not sat up and unravelled everything: instead his body had *passed through* the material.

Now the other disciple steps into the tomb and sees what Peter has seen. Because this is eye-witness evidence from John, we can hear him telling us what happened next: *I saw and believed* (see 8b).

The tomb was empty.

2. – Jesus appeared (11-18)

Peter and John have left (see 10), so Mary Magdalene is on her own outside the tomb.

As she looks inside the tomb she sees two angels, but it looks like she does not realise who they are: she can't see clearly because of her tears. When they ask her why she is crying she replies *They have taken my Lord away... and I don't know where they have put him* (13b).

At this, Mary turns round and sees someone standing there, *but she did not realise that it was Jesus* (14b). So she asks the man, who she assumes is the gardener, where Jesus is (see 15).

Jesus said to her, 'Mary' (16a).

Did he say it the way Jesus always said her name? Suddenly she *knows*: it's Jesus.

Mary must have moved towards Jesus to embrace him, because he says *Do not hold on to me, for I have not yet ascended to my Father* (17a). What's going on here? Surely it is that Mary must begin to learn to relate to Jesus in a new way, because he is going back to glory.

Instead he gives her a job to do. She is to go and give the disciples his message: *I am ascending to my Father and your Father, to my God and your God* (17b). If he had said *our Father and our God* that would have blurred the distinction between Jesus and his friends, so Jesus chooses his words carefully.

So Mary runs off to pass on the news to the disciples. The key thing she tells them is that *I have seen the Lord!* (18a) The risen Jesus has appeared to her.

3. – The disciples were transformed (19-29)

Most of the disciples had deserted Jesus at his arrest, and yet a few weeks later they were willing to risk their lives to tell the world the good news about him.

Something must have happened: instead of running for their lives, they started living for their Master. The most plausible explanation for this transformation is the resurrection of Jesus.

John remembers what happened: *Jesus came and stood among them and said 'Peace be with you!'* (19b) That brings the transformation.

First, fear turns to joy.

The disciples are together, *with the doors locked for fear of the Jewish leaders* (19).

But when Jesus appears two things convince the disciples that he has risen: he gets into the room despite those locked doors, and *he showed them his hands and side* (20). So, says John, *the disciples were overjoyed when they saw the Lord* (20b).

Second, guilt turns to forgiveness.

The disciples probably feel bad for letting Jesus down, but he is sending them out with a message: *As the Father has sent me, I am sending you* (21b).

So Jesus breathes on them and says *Receive the Holy Spirit. If you forgive anyone's sins, their sins are forgiven; if you do not forgive them, they are not forgiven* (22b-23).

Jesus is repeating his promise to the disciples in the Upper Room to send his Spirit, but now he is reinforcing it by breathing on them. And on the basis of the message they will proclaim – about his death and resurrection – Jesus is giving the disciples the right to declare whether someone is forgiven or not.

And this authority is ours too: if someone trusts in what Jesus did on the cross, they are forgiven; and if they don't, they aren't. Faith in the crucified and risen Jesus turns guilt to forgiveness.

And, *third*, doubt turns to faith.

Thomas wasn't there when Jesus came to the disciples. So when they tell him that they have met Jesus he is very sceptical: *Unless I see the nail marks in his hands and put my finger where the nails were, and put my hand into his side, I will not believe* (25b).

Thomas spends the next week (see 26a) wondering if his friends have got it wrong. But he must also be thinking *If Jesus really has risen from the dead, that means he has the authority to forgive sins and is the Son of God.*

And then Jesus comes. He gets through the locked doors again (see 26) and tells Thomas to do precisely what Thomas had said he'd need to do to be able to believe (see 27a): he knows exactly what his sceptical friend has been saying.

But Thomas doesn't need to see the scars or touch the wounds. He looks at Jesus and says *My Lord and my God!* (28) Thomas is changed for ever: doubt has turned to faith.

But Jesus has something to say to him, and to us too: *Because you have seen me, you have believed; blessed are those who have not seen and yet have believed* (29).

Faith means hearing the disciples' message that they have *seen* the risen Jesus, weighing up the evidence, and deciding to trust Jesus for ourselves.

A key part of that evidence is the transformation of the disciples.

One purpose (20:30-31)

John has told us about twelve Jesus signs – two in each section of his Gospel. But there were *many other signs* too which Jesus also performed *in the presence of his disciples* (30; and see, for example, chapter 21:1-14).

So why did John write his book?

These are written that you may believe that Jesus is the Messiah, the Son of God, and that by believing you may have life in his name (31).

John has introduced us to people who have come to *believe* in Jesus: Nathanael (1:49), the Samaritans (4:42), the man born blind (9:38), Martha (11:27), the disciples in general (16:30) and Thomas in particular (20:28).

He is inviting us to put *our* faith in Jesus, too. And he reminds us that as we do that, we will *have life in his name* (31b).

Learning the Gospel

For most of us, learning the second half of Section Six will be easier than learning the first half, as we are more familiar with it.

Once again, first learn the main headings, which are in bold. Only then, and taking each part in turn (first Block Z, then Sign A and so on), learn the sub-headings. Feel free to change these if you can improve on them.

If you work at this for a few minutes, and repeat the process later, it will not take you long to learn.

Section Six: The Love (second half)

Three blocks

X. Jesus and his friends

Y. Jesus and his Father
(Blocks X and Y belong to the first half of Section Six.)

Z. Jesus and his enemies
1. Jesus arrested
2. Jesus denied
3. Jesus condemned

Two signs

A. The crucifixion

1. See him crucified
2. Hear him die
3. Respond to his love

B. The resurrection

1. The tomb was empty
2. Jesus appeared
3. The disciples were transformed

One purpose

Meeting the Lord

The danger with this second half of Section Six is that we neglect it because we know the story already. But the two signs here, and what leads up to them, are the foundation of our faith.

The cross is where we meet Jesus and find forgiveness, which the empty tomb confirms.

So let me encourage you to start telling yourself the events of Block Z (it may be best to do it aloud). Include the details which occur to you, but don't beat yourself up about those which don't. Doing this with a friend will make it more enjoyable.

Then you might want to look at the text again and pick up on any details you have missed.

Now do the same with Sign A, and then Sign B.

As you tell yourself/each other the story, be always ready to start praying: thank Jesus for his astonishing love and worship him.

As you re-tell John you will be rediscovering Jesus.

John's Conclusion (John 21:1-25)

Most conclusions simply finish off a story: they are often something of an anticlimax. But John's is different.

Enjoying the View

A. The end of the past (21:1-14)

1. The decision (1-3)
2. The revelation (4-8)
3. The encounter (9-14)

B. The start of the future (21:15-25)

1. The reinstatement (15-17)
2. The priority (18-23)
3. The Gospel (24-25)

John's conclusion, like his introduction, clearly has two parts.

In the first, John looks *back* and tells us how the story of Jesus and his disciples ends: at Lake Galilee, with another sign and with breakfast on the beach.

In the second half of his conclusion, John looks *forward* and gives us a hint of the story to come.

The reason is simple. As we heard Jesus say in the Upper Room, he is going away, which in one sense is the end of the story. But he is also sending his Spirit, who will work through the disciples so that a new story can begin.

So John's conclusion is also an introduction.

It would be good to read through this last chapter of John's Gospel. Try to imagine the emotions of the seven disciples in the first half, and Peter's emotions in the second half.

Unpacking the Content

A. The end of the past (21:1-14)

This is the last *sign* in John's Gospel.

1. – The decision (1-3)

It's Peter who takes the lead: *I'm going out to fish* (3a). And the other six disciples agree to go with him.

There is no suggestion that this was a bad decision. Jesus had sent a message to the disciples that they should go to Galilee where he would meet them (see Mark 14:28).

So they are there (see 1) and they are waiting. It's natural that Peter thinks they might as well do something useful in the meantime.

But things don't go well, because *that night they caught nothing* (3b).

2. – The revelation (4-8)

In the early morning comes the *sign*. On hearing that they haven't caught anything, a man on the shore calls out to them: *Throw your net on the right side of the boat and you will find some fish* (6a).

Now John tells us that when the disciples follow his advice, they are *unable to haul the net in because of the large number of fish* (6b).

While they are recovering from their surprise, John (*the disciple whom Jesus loved*) says *It is the Lord!* (7a)

Try to imagine the scene.

Does John recognise the man on the shore because this fish miracle reminds him of another one when they were first getting to know Jesus (see Luke 5:4-7)? Or is he just living in the expectation that their friend and Lord could come to meet them at any moment?

So Peter does the Peter thing and plunges into the water: time is of the essence (see 7b). I can't prove it, but I don't think he's doing this to see if John is right; I think he *knows*.

So while Peter is wading in towards the shore his heart is pounding with excitement.

Once again, a sign has pointed to the identity of Jesus. It's a revelation.

3. – The encounter (9-14)

When they reach land, the disciples see *a fire of burning coals there with fish on it, and some bread* (9). And Jesus says *Come and have breakfast* (12a).

John paints a picture of the mixture of bewilderment and joy on the shore that morning: *None of the disciples dared ask him 'Who are you?' They knew it was the Lord* (12b).

And so they have breakfast with their Creator.

John puts this encounter in context for us: *This was now the third time Jesus appeared to his disciples after he was raised from the dead* (14; we saw the first two appearances in chapter 20:19-23 and 20:24-29).

Jesus had begun his story with the disciples by calling them and telling them that they would one day fish for people (see Mark 1:17). This last sign is a reminder that the one who is sending them out into the world is the master fisherman.

B. The start of the future (21:15-25)

This passage looks forwards, to what will happen after the end of chapter 21.

1. – The reinstatement (15-17)

It looks like this conversation between Jesus and Peter takes place as the two of them are walking along the shore after breakfast (see 20a).

So Jesus asks his question: *Simon son of John, do you love me more than these?* (15a)

More than what? My guess is that Jesus is reminding Peter that he had claimed to have greater love for Jesus than the other disciples: *Even if all fall away, I will not* (Mark 14:29).

Jesus asks his question three times, and John tells us that because of this *Peter was hurt* (17). The reason must be the denial while Jesus was being interrogated (see chapter 18:15-18, 25-27).

Peter must have been thinking about his three-times denial of Jesus during their breakfast together. And now here is Jesus not only asking him *Do you love me?* but asking him *three times*.

It's all flooding back to him: the guilt, the shame.

But Jesus isn't asking the love question to *humiliate* Peter but to *reinstate* him: *Feed my lambs* (15b; and see 16b, 17b).

Peter's new story is just starting: he is to provide spiritual nourishment to those who will believe in Jesus.

2. – The priority (18-23)

Jesus tells Peter that one day *you will stretch out your hands and someone else will dress you and lead you where you do not want to go* (18b).

We don't know if Peter understood what Jesus was getting at, but John leaves us in no doubt: *Jesus said this to indicate the kind of death by which Peter would glorify God* (19a).

Peter, like his Lord, would be crucified.

In the meantime, says Jesus, *Follow me!* (19b) This is to be Peter's priority.

But Peter changes the subject. Because of his close friendship with John, he wants to know about *his* future: *Lord, what about him?* (21)

Jesus more or less says to Peter that he is to mind his own business. And his own business is clear: *You must follow me* (22b).

Following Jesus is to be the priority for all of us who have become his disciples.

3. – The Gospel (24-25)

John ends his Gospel by passing on the opinion of others as to the reliability of the story he has told: *We know that his testimony is true* (24b). Some think that this is the leaders of the church in Ephesus giving John's Gospel their seal of approval.

So John the Gospel-writer reminds us that *Jesus did many other things as well* (25a). In other words, everything in this book is here *by selection*. And, as Jesus promised in Section Six, the Holy Spirit has been guiding John throughout the process (see chapter 14:26 and 16:13-14).

The new story continues after the end of chapter 21. You and I are part of it.

And the Holy Spirit wants to use John's Gospel, both in our lives and in the lives of others, so that glory comes to God.

Learning the Gospel

First, learn the two headings in bold. Then, second, learn the subheadings.

I repeat what I have said so often during the course of our journey through John's Gospel: this isn't difficult, and it's worth it.

John's Conclusion

A. The end of the past
1. The decision
2. The revelation
3. The encounter

B. The start of the future
1. The reinstatement
2. The priority
3. The Gospel

Meeting the Lord

This is a reminder, once again, of why we are doing this: we want to get to know Jesus better.

So, without a Bible, start to tell yourself the story of the miraculous catch of fish. As you use the sub-headings you will remember many of the details (but don't beat yourself up about those you have forgotten!).

As you do this, you will find yourself praying. Thank Jesus for what he has done in your life to reveal himself to you, and ask him to keep doing it. You might also want to pray for friends of yours who would not yet count themselves as believers.

Now do the same thing with the second half of the passage. As you do so, you will be getting to know Jesus better.

There is nothing more important than that.

My Conclusion:
The Experiment goes on

I hope you have taken time on your way through *The John Experiment* to learn the structure of the Gospel.

If you have, you have heard Jesus announcing the message that he is like new wine replacing old religion; you have seen his authority in action in extraordinary healings and in teaching about his unique relationship with God the Father; you have watched him training his disciples as he has answered his critics and declared himself to be the the bread, the water and the light every human being needs.

You have seen him raise a dead man to life, heard his opponents plotting his death, and seen what it costs those who decide to follow him; you have heard him invite everyone to trust in him and so avoid God's judgment; and you have seen his astonishing love in promising to send the Holy Spirit to his disciples and in going to the cross to die for our sins.

And by seeing his empty tomb, his appearing to Mary Magdalene, and his transformed disciples, you have had the opportunity to acknowledge him as the risen Lord.

I hope you have begun to rediscover Jesus.

But that process doesn't need to stop because you have reached the end of this book. I want to suggest a few ways in which you can keep using John's Gospel to get to know Jesus better.

1. Using John's Gospel for worship and prayer

Take one section of John. As you begin to run through it in your mind (without your Bible!), don't just remember the order of the signs and blocks: talk to Jesus about what he is doing and saying. Enjoy spending time with him. Worship him for his power and his love. And pray for yourself as you think your way through the section.

You can do this at home in your room, or while you are sitting on the bus. You might decide to use Section One this way for a week; the following week you could move on to Section Two.

2. Using John's Gospel to help you pray for others

Sometimes you want to pray for a friend or for a member of your family, but you're not sure how. Why not take one section of the Gospel and pray through it, praying the whole time for this special person?

With some incidents you will be praying that she will recognize more and more who Jesus is and why he came; sometimes you will be praying that she will *experience* the rivers of living water of the Holy Spirit; sometimes you will pray that the message of the cross will move her as never before.

The Gospel can help you pray for others, whether these people are already Christians or not.

3. Using John's Gospel for a John Walk

Go for a walk (without a Bible) with a friend who has learnt the same section(s) of John as you have. Take turns to tell each other the signs and the blocks, including as many details as you can remember. This is not a competition: you can help one another as you re-tell John.

When you get home you might take some time to thank Jesus and worship Jesus together. (You might also want to turn to John's Gospel to remind yourselves of any details neither of you could remember.)

The John Walk works well with a group too. But however you do it, it is so healthy to be using John's Gospel to help you talk about Jesus!

4. Using John's Gospel in a teaching programme

Your youth group or student group might decide to use the structure of John in its term programme. At your first meeting you could look at John's Introduction, at your second meeting Section One, and so on.

Different small groups could look at the different signs and blocks and then share with everyone what they have learnt. And some of the group might decide to learn the structure of the week's section for themselves, so that they can get to know Jesus better.

This could work well, too, in a church's Sunday teaching programme. The first sermon in a series could be on chapter 1 (John's Introduction). Then you could have one or two sermons on each of the six sections in turn.

5. Using John's Gospel in a house group

It is possible to study the whole of John's Gospel – and to learn it too! – in a house group context. There are suggested outlines for such a series in Appendix 2.

Finally...

Thank you for reading *The John Experiment*.

Being a Christian is about much more than just believing a message: it's about trusting Jesus, the Messiah and the Son of God (see chapter 20:31). The Holy Spirit is living inside every Christian, and he loves to use his word to *change* us.

Please pray for yourself, and for others trying the John experiment, that all of us will love and experience Jesus more.

That way we will bring glory to God. And that is *life* (see chapter 20:31).

Appendix 1:
Questions about John's Gospel

Below are some of the questions I have most often been asked about John's Gospel. I can only comment briefly here: to learn more, please go to the larger commentaries. And, of course, I am still learning!

1. Why is John's Gospel so different from the others?

Here are just a few of the differences: John's Introduction (especially chapter 1:1-18) is not at all like the beginning of Matthew, Mark and Luke; and John includes no parables to speak of. John also recounts a number of events which are not to be found in any of the other Gospels.

But the biggest difference is this: while the other Gospel-writers record Jesus visiting Jerusalem only once (for the climactic events of the cross and the resurrection), John tells us of regular trips by Jesus to Jerusalem.

None of these differences amounts to a contradiction. It looks like John has simply decided to tell the Jesus story differently. It may also be that he is more concerned about getting the order of the events right than Matthew, Mark and Luke are: for example, see his regular use of *After this...* and similar expressions (see chapter 2:12; 3:22; 4:43; 5:1; 6:1,22; 7:1; 12:12; 17:1; 18:1; 21:1).

2. Who says John's Gospel has a structure at all?

I can't prove that it has, but it seems to me to make sense.

In a culture in which you couldn't print off copies of books, it strikes me that writing a book with a memorable structure is the obvious thing to do. As John was writing something he considered incredibly important, he wanted people to pass it on to others: if they could learn the order of the events off by heart, that's exactly what they could do.

3. Who says my structure of John's Gospel is the right one?

Well, certainly not me.

There are lots of suggested structures of John, and it's a brave Bible teacher who claims they have found *the* right one.

But what I *am* saying about this structure is that it is *regular*: there are two signs and three blocks in each section. And that means that it's easier to learn.

And John seems to have deliberately put the two signs in each section *together* (except in Section Four): the two signs at the beginning of Section Two, for example, are together (see chapter 4:43 - 5:15), even though four months probably separate chapter 4 from chapter 5.

If my structure of John's Gospel is not *John's* structure of John's Gospel, that doesn't bother me. I am not using this structure to teach some weird and wonderful new doctrine: if you've read the book you will see that what I have been trying to do is simply teach through John's Gospel.

But in such a way that you can commit it to memory.

4. Aren't there 7 signs in John's Gospel?

Many of the commentaries I've looked at say there are 7 signs: it's a kind of Christian magic number.

But John himself only describes three incidents in his Gospel as *signs*. These are the two miracles in Cana (see chapter 2:11 and 4:54) and the feeding of the 5,000 (see chapter 6:14, but see also chapter 9:16).

But those who believe there are 7 signs in John cannot agree as to which they are. Everyone accepts the following 6 signs: the wedding at Cana, the healing of the royal official's son, the healing of the paralysed man at the Pool Bethesda, the feeding of the 5,000, the healing of the man born blind, and the raising of Lazarus.

But is the 7th sign Jesus walking on the water, the miraculous catch of fish in chapter 21, or the resurrection of Jesus?

However, I see no reason why *sign* has to mean *miracle*. Just because every miracle is a sign, that doesn't mean that every sign is a miracle, does it?

5. When was John's Gospel written?

Nearly everyone agrees that Mark's Gospel was the first to be written (in the 60s), and John's Gospel the last. Many would say John wrote in the 80s or the 90s. And perhaps they are right.

But John 5:2 may be a hint that the Gospel was written *before* the destruction of Jerusalem by the Romans in AD70. Talking about the Pool Bethesda, John tells his readers that there *is* a pool in Jerusalem. Not *was*, but *is*.

I find that intriguing.

6. What is the relationship between John's Gospel and Mark's Gospel?

There is evidence that John expected that some, perhaps many, of his readers would already have heard Mark's version of the Jesus story.

Here is the clue that I find the most convincing. In chapter 3:23 John tells us that John the Baptist was baptising at a place called Aenon. Then he adds: *This was before John was put in prison* (24).

Isn't that a strange thing to write? If John is baptising, it's *obvious* that he isn't in prison, isn't it? What's going on here?

The only explanation for John to have written chapter 3:24 is that he reckons that a number of readers will read about John baptising and think of Mark 1:14, which begins *After John was put in prison...* They will be saying to themselves *How can John the Baptist still be baptising people? Surely he's in prison, isn't he?*

So by writing John 3:24, John is saying to all those people who know Mark's Gospel: *Everything I've written so far in my Gospel happened before Mark 1:14. The wedding at Cana, the judgment in the temple and Jesus' conversation with Nicodemus – these all happened between Mark 1:13 and Mark 1:14.*

I cannot think of another explanation.

(For more on this question, see Richard Bauckham, *John for Readers of Mark*, in *The Gospels for All Christians*, pp147-171, Eerdmans 1998.)

7. Which is my favourite commentary on John's Gospel?

While I have learnt from many John commentaries, the one I am most impressed by and have used most is IVP's Tyndale New Testament Commentary by Colin Kruse. Of course we will all find different books on John's Gospel helpful, but for my money this one wins easily.

Colin G Kruse, *John: An Introduction and Commentary*, Inter-Varsity Press 2003.

Appendix 2:
The John Experiment in a House Group

The following series of studies has 9 sessions and is designed for group use; but of course you could also use these questions for your own study or one-to-one with a friend.

These questions are designed for people who have already read the relevant section in *The John Experiment*. In a house group it might make sense if everyone reads the whole passage in John's Gospel before coming to the meeting: this will save significant time.

It is up to you whether you combine answering the questions with learning the order of the events!

9 Weeks in John's Gospel

Week One
John's Introduction (John 1:1-51)

Read chapter 1:1-18

1. What is Jesus' relationship with God? And with John the Baptist?

2. What does this passage tell us about what the right response to Jesus is?

3. Take a moment for everyone to choose their favourite verse from John 1:1-18. Then share your choices and explain them, too.

Read chapter 1:19-51

4. What is there here to show that John the Baptist thinks Jesus is incredibly important?

5. How could we describe each of the people Jesus calls to follow him? Which one do we identify most with?

6. What do we think Jesus means in verse 51 when he says that the angels will ascend and descend on the Son of Man?

7. How do we think John the Baptist felt when two of his disciples left and started following Jesus (see verse 37)? Why?

8. How could we describe Jesus in this second half of John's Introduction? How are we going to respond to him?

Do any of us know the order of the events in John's Introduction? Or would any of us like to?

Week Two
Section One: The Message (John 2:1 - 4:42)

Read all of chapter 2

1. How do we know the story of the wedding at Cana is not simply about Jesus helping people out in a tricky situation?

2. What is the message of these two signs when you put them together? Is that still a relevant message today?

Read chapter 3:1 - 4:42

3. In what way does Jesus' message to Nicodemus fit with the signs in chapter 2?

4. Read Ezekiel 36:25-27, which is a passage Nicodemus will have known very well. Why should he have understood what Jesus said about being born again?

5. Look at chapter 3:22-36. What's the most important thing for John the Baptist? And for John the Gospel-writer?

6. Let's see if we can see how the Samaritan woman changes her mind during chapter 4 as to who Jesus is.

7. Why do we think the Samaritans from her town were so excited about Jesus? Why is verse 42 so important?

8. Let's make a list of things we've learnt from Section One which are part of the message we want to share with others.

Do any of us know the order of the events in Section One? Or would any of us like to?

Week Three
Section Two: The Authority (John 4:43 - 5:47)

Read chapter 4:43 - 5:15

1. What are some of the similarities between these two signs? And what are the differences?

2. Why do the religious leaders get so upset with Jesus?

Read chapter 5:16-47

3. What is Jesus claiming about himself? Is he saying that he's a second God?

4. Why has God the Father given Jesus the responsibility of being the judge on Judgment Day (see verses 22-23)?

5. How would we explain verse 24 to an 8 year-old?

6. Why does Jesus say people should believe in him (see verses 31-40)?

7. What does Jesus accuse the religious leaders of (see verses 41-47)?

8. In what ways could we describe Jesus after watching him and listening to him in Section Two?

Do any of us know the order of the events in Section Two? Or would any of us like to?

Week Four
Section Three: The Training (John 6:1 - 8:59)

Read chapter 6:1-24

1. Why did the crowd want to make Jesus king after he had fed the 5,000 (see verses 14-15)?

2. What do we think Jesus was teaching the disciples by walking on Lake Galilee?

Read chapter 6:25-71

3. What do we think the crowds found it hardest to hear when Jesus was teaching?

Read chapter 7:1-52

4. Let's make a list of the negative opinions of Jesus in this chapter. And then of the positive opinions.

5. Let's read verses 50-52 again. What do we think it cost Nicodemus to say what he says here? And why did he say it?

Read chapter 8:12-59

6. Jesus tells the crowd they are wrong about themselves. What things does he point to in particular (see veses 31-47)?

7. What is Jesus claiming in verse 58? And do we think he is doing this deliberately? Why does he do it?

8. Imagine that we are the disciples listening to Jesus. What will we have learnt about him in Section Three?

Do any of us know the order of the events in Section Three? Or would any of us like to?

Week Five
Section Four: The Cost (John 9:1 - 11:57)

Read the whole of chapter 9

1. Why do we think the Pharisees are so determined not to believe in Jesus?

2. Can we find the verses which show the healed man's growing under-standing of who Jesus is? What does this cost him?

Read the whole of chapter 10

3. What is Jesus teaching here by describing himself as the good shep-herd?

4. What does Jesus say in chapter 10 about who he is and about why he has come into the world?

Read the whole of chapter 11:1-44

5. Why doesn't Jesus go to heal Lazarus as soon as he hears he's ill?

6. What difference does it make if someone believes that Jesus is the resurrection and the life?

Read chapter 11:45-57

7. What do we think is the most important thing in the verses we've just read?

8. If we had just read Section Four for the first time, how might we de-scribe Jesus?

Do any of us know the order of the events in Section Four? Or would any of us like to?

Week Six
Section Five: The Judgment (John 12:1-50)

Read chapter 12:1-19

1. Why do we think John tells us about the anointing at Bethany? And is the reaction important when Jesus comes into Jerusalem?

2. How do we think Jesus felt when Mary anointed him? And how did he feel when the crowd in Jerusalem started cheering?

3. Which of these two incidents would you have liked to be at? Why?

Read chapter 12:20-36

4. Why do we think Jesus knows that the time has come for him to go to the cross (see verse 23)?

5. Why do we think God the Father chooses to speak from heaven in verse 28? And what does this tell us about the relationship between God the Father and God the Son?

Read chapter 12:37-50

6. Why does Jesus say so many people reject him?

7. Let's look at verses 44-50. What is Jesus offering everyone who trusts him?

8. As we get to the end of Section Five, how do we think Jesus is feeling? And how are *we* feeling about Jesus?

Do any of us know the order of the events in Section Five? Or would any of us like to?

Week Seven
Section Six (first half): The Love (John 13:1 - 17:26)

Read the whole of chapter 13

1. In what way is the footwashing a preview of the cross and the resurrection of Jesus? How can we obey Jesus' command to love each other?

Read the whole of chapter 14

2. What does Jesus mean when he calls himself the way, the truth and the life?

3. In the second half of the chapter Jesus promises his disciples the Holy Spirit. What good will he do them? And us?

Read chapter 15:1 - 16:3

4. What three relationships does Jesus talk about in this chapter? Why do we think he picks on these three?

5. Get into three small groups. Each group looks at one of the relationships and answers these questions: Why is it important? And what

practical step can we take to obey Jesus? (Then share with the whole group.)

Read chapter 16:4-33

6. What three things will the Holy Spirit do for all believers in Jesus? Why is each of them important?

Read the whole of chapter 17

7. Why do we think Jesus feels it necessary to pray like this before he goes to the cross?

8. Try and work out what are the three most important things he prays for us. Which is the most important for each of us?

9. Jesus takes a lot of trouble to prepare the disciples for what is to come. What is the thing Jesus teaches in these chapters which is most important to you personally? Why? (Think about this in silence; then share with the whole group.)

Do any of us know the order of the events in the first half of Section Six? Or would any of us like to?

Week Eight
Section Six (second half): The Love (John 18:1 - 20:31)

Read chapter 18:1 - 19:16

1. Let's pick out some things here which show that Jesus is determined to go to the cross.

2. How would we describe Pilate's reaction to Jesus? Do we think a lot of people are like that today?

Read chapter 19:17-42

3. Why do we think Pilate is so obstinate about the notice on the cross? And why do we think it matters?

4. How would we explain to an 8 year-old what Jesus meant when he said *It is finished*?

5. What do we think it was which made Joseph want to show Pilate that he cared about Jesus?

Read chapter 20:1-29

6. What three pieces of evidence does John give us that Jesus has risen from the dead? Which do we find most convincing?

7. Do we think Thomas was right or wrong not to believe Jesus had risen from the dead until he saw him for himself?

8. How would we explain the two parts of Thomas' exclamation in verse 28 to an 8 year-old?

Read chapter 20:30-31

9. What does someone need to do in order to get real life through Jesus?

Do any of us know the order of the events in the second half of Section Six? Or would any of us like to?

Week Nine
John's Conclusion (John 21:1-25)

Read verses 1-14

1. How do we think the disciples were feeling in verse 3? And in verse 6? And in verse 12?

Read verses 15-23

2. Why do we think Jesus asked Peter three times if he loved him?

3. What do we think Jesus means when he tells Peter to feed his lambs or his sheep? Is this something just for Peter, or for all of us?

Read verses 24 and 25

4. Without mentioning the cross or the resurrection of Jesus, each of us writes down the three things in John's Gospel which have impacted them most. Then let's share our answers.

5. Why are the cross and the resurrection the most important parts of the Christian message?

6. What does John's Gospel give us that the other Gospels don't? What excites us most about John's book?

7. How has reading about Jesus in John's Gospel *changed* us? How would we *like* it to change us?

8. How can we pray for each other so that we will be serious about following Jesus?

Do any of us know the order of the events in John's Conclusion? Or would any of us like to?

Do any of us know the order of the events in all of John's Gospel? Would any of us like to?

Appendix 3:
The Structure of John's Gospel

John's Introduction (John 1:1-51)

A. Jesus: the Word of God (1:1-18)
  a. The supremacy of Jesus (1-5)
  b. John the Baptist and Jesus (6-8)
  c. Reactions to Jesus (9-14)
  b'. John the Baptist and Jesus (15)
  a'. The supremacy of Jesus (16-18)

B. Jesus: who is this man? (1:19-51)
  1. What Isaiah says (19-28)
  2. What John says (29-34)
  3. What Andrew says (35-42)
  4. What Nathanael says (43-49)
  5. What Jesus says (50-51)

Section One: The Message (John 2:1 - 4:42)

Two signs

A. The wedding at Cana (2:1-12)
  1. Jesus the guest (1-5)
  2. Jesus the host (6-10)
  3. Reaction: real faith (11-12)

B. Judgment in the temple (2:13-25)
  1. Jesus judges the temple (13-17)
  2. Jesus replaces the temple (18-22)
  3. Reaction: superficial faith (23-25)

Three blocks

X. Jesus and Nicodemus (3:1-21)
  1. What the Spirit does (3-10)
  2. What the Son says (11-15)
  3. What the Father offers (16-21)

Y. The truth about Jesus (3:22-36)

1. What John the Baptist says (22-30)
2. What John the Gospel-writer says (31-36)

Z. Jesus and the Samaritan woman (4:1-42)

1. He's a Jew (7-9)
2. He's greater than Jacob (10-15)
3. He's a prophet (16-24)
4. He's the Messiah (25-42)

Section Two: The Authority (John 4:43 - 5:47)

Two signs

A. Jesus heals a royal official's son (4:43-54)

1. Great need (46-47)
2. Effortless authority (48-50a)
3. Growing faith (50b-54)

B. Jesus heals a paralysed man (5:1-15)

1. Great need (1-3)
2. Effortless authority (5-9a)
3. Growing opposition (9b-15)

Three blocks

X. The claim (5:16-30)

a. Jesus and the Father (19-20a)
b. Jesus the life-giver (20b-21)
c. Jesus the judge (22-23)
d. Jesus and us (24)
c'. Jesus the judge (25-27)
b'. Jesus the life-giver (28-29)
a'. Jesus and the Father (30)

Y. The evidence (5:31-40)

1. What John says (31-35)
2. What Jesus does (36)
3. What Scripture says (37-40)

Z. The diagnosis (5:41-47)

1. They don't love God (41-44)
2. They don't believe Moses (45-47)

Section Three: The Training (John 6:1 - 8:59)

Two signs

A. Jesus feeds the 5,000 (6:1-15)

1. The situation (1-4)
2. The miracle (5-13)
3. The reaction (14-15)

B. Jesus walks on Lake Galilee (6:16-24)

1. The situation (16-18)
2. The miracle (19-21)
3. The reaction (22-24)

Three blocks

X. Jesus: the bread of life (6:25-71)

1. His diagnosis (25-34)
2. His claim (35-48)
3. His explanation (49-59)
4. His question (60-71)

Y. Jesus: the source of water (7:1-52)

1. Jesus' authority (10-24)
2. Jesus' identity (25-36)
3. Jesus' promise (37-44)

Z. Jesus: the light of the world (8:12-59)

1. Jesus' authority (12-30)
2. What Jesus thinks of the crowd (31-47)
3. What the crowd think of Jesus (48-59)

Section Four: The Cost (John 9:1 - 11:57)

Sign A. Jesus heals a man born blind (9:1-41)

1. The healing (1-12)
2. The investigation (13-34)
3. The decision (35-41)

Block X. Jesus: the good shepherd (10:1-21)

a. The parable (1-6)
b. Jesus is the door (7-10)
b'. Jesus is the shepherd (11-18)
a'. The reaction (19-21)

Block Y. Jesus: who is this man? (10:22-42)

1. Jesus is the Messiah (22-30)
2. Jesus is the Son of God (31-39)

Sign B. Jesus raises Lazarus from death (11:1-44)

1. Trust his plan (1-16)
2. Hear his claim (17-27)
3. See his tears (28-37)
4. Experience his power (38-44)

Block Z. Jesus: this man must die (11:45-57)

1. What Caiaphas says (45-53)
2. What Jesus does (54-57)

Section Five: The Judgment (John 12:1-50)

Two signs

A. The anointing in Bethany (12:1-11)

1. What Mary does (1-3)
2. How Judas reacts (4-6)
3. What Jesus says (7-8)

B. The arrival in Jerusalem (12:12-19)

1. The arrival (12-13)
2. The meaning (14-15)
3. The reaction (16-19)

Three blocks

X. The decision (12:20-36)

1. Jesus (20-26)
2. The Father (27-33)
3. The crowd (34-36)

Y. The rejection (12:37-43)

1. The surprise (37)
2. The explanation (38-41)
3. The reaction (42-43)

Z. The invitation (12:44-50)

1. The necessity of faith (44-46)
2. The certainty of judgment (47-48)
3. The message of the Son (49-50)

Section Six: The Love (John 13:1 - 20:31)

Three blocks

X. Jesus and his friends (13:1 - 16:33)

1. The last supper (13:1-38)

a. Jesus: his love (1-5)
b. Peter: his objection (6-11)
c. Disciples: our task (12-17)
b'. Judas: his betrayal (18-30)
a'. Jesus: his command to love (31-35)

2. The last teaching (14:1 - 16:33)

a. Jesus: he's leaving (14:1-14)
   i.   He is the way (1-5)
   ii. He is the truth (7-11)
   iii. He is the life (12-14)

b. The Spirit: he's coming (14:15-31)
   i.   Love for the soul (18-24)
   ii. Truth for the world (25-26)
   iii. Peace for the heart (27-31)

   c. Disciples: our priorities (15:1 - 16:3)
- i.   The relationship to Jesus (1-11)
- ii.   The relationship to one another (12-17)
- iii. The relationship to the world (15:18 - 16:3)

   b'. The Spirit: he's coming (16:4-15)
- i.   He brings the presence of Jesus (4-7)
- ii.   He spreads the message of Jesus (8-11)
- iii. He completes the revelation of Jesus (12-15)

   a'. Jesus: he's leaving (16:16-33)
- i.   He promises them joy (19-24)
- ii.   He reminds them of love (25-28)
- iii. He offers them peace (29-33)

Y. Jesus and his Father (17:1-26)

1. Jesus prays for himself (1-5)
2. Jesus prays for the apostles (6-19)
3. Jesus prays for us (20-26)

Z. Jesus and his enemies (18:1 - 19:16)

1. Jesus arrested (18:1-14)
2. Jesus denied (18:15-27)
3. Jesus condemned (18:28 - 19:16)

Two signs

A. The crucifixion (19:17-42)

1. See him crucified (17-27)
2. Hear him die (28-30)
3. Respond to his love (31-42)

B. The resurrection (20:1-29)

1. The tomb was empty (1-10)
2. Jesus appeared (11-18)
3. The disciples were transformed (19-29)

One purpose (20:30-31)

John's Conclusion (John 21:1-25)

A. The end of the past (21:1-14)

1. The decision (1-3)
2. The revelation (4-8)
3. The encounter (9-14)

B. The start of the future (21:15-25)

1. The reinstatement (15-17)
2. The priority (18-23)
3. The Gospel (24-25)

How to Teach the Bible
so that People Meet God

Andrew Page

Andrew Page believes that Bible teaching can be a supernatural event. A graduate of London School of Theology, Andrew was a missionary in Austria for 20 years, working with the Austrian Christian student movement (IFES) and later pastoring a church in Innsbruck.

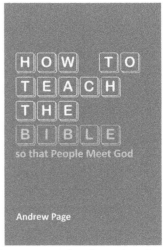

He says "Two enemies of Christian churches are Bible teaching with little biblical content and Bible teaching which is more a lecture than an event." If you agree with this, *How to Teach the Bible so that People Meet God* is the book for you.

This is unashamedly a how-to book. Andrew has trained others in this method of teaching a Bible passage in a number of countries around Europe, and now for the first time the method is available as a book.

So, 3 questions before you buy this book:
• Do you want to find out if God has given you the gift of teaching?
• Do you want to grow in the gift you believe you have?
• Do you want to help a friend to develop as a Bible teacher?

If you have said *Yes* to any of these questions, *How to Teach the Bible so that People Meet God* is a great place to start.

ISBN 978-3-95776-035-7
Pb. • 64 pp. • £ 7.50

VTR Publications
info@vtr-online.com
http://www.vtr-online.com

The 5 Habits of
Deeply Contented People

Andrew Page

Have you found contentment?
Most people are looking for it.
If you're not, it may be because you've given up...

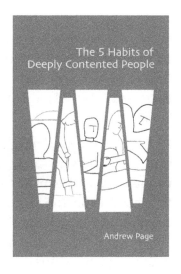

If you are searching or want to start your search again, *The 5 Habits of Deeply Contented People* is the book for you.

The Bible says that everyone is made in God's image. Andrew Page says there are 5 habits which express that image of God in us. He says "If we can work out what these habits mean in practice for us as individuals, we will experience a deeper level of contentment."

Basing what he writes on the second chapter of the Bible, and making clear that these habits work even if we don't believe in God, Andrew invites his readers to try out the habits for themselves.

• Do you want to be more contented, whatever life throws at you?
• Are you curious to know what it means to be made in God's image?
• Would you like to find out if the 5 habits work?

If you have said Yes to any of these questions, *The 5 Habits of Deeply Contented People* is a great place to start.

ISBN 978-3-95776-009-8
Pb. • 52 pp. • £ 7.00

VTR Publications
info@vtr-online.com
http://www.vtr-online.com

The Mark Experiment

How Mark's Gospel can help you know Jesus better

Andrew Page

If you are looking for a new way into Mark's Gospel and you long to allow the Gospel to help you worship and experience Jesus, *The Mark Experiment* is the book for you.

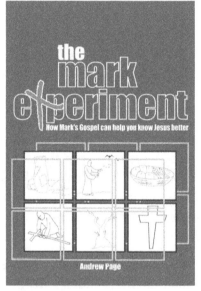

In *The Mark Experiment* Andrew Page shows you how to commit the Gospel to memory and explains how learning to meditate on the Gospel events has transformed his relationship with Jesus. Think what this might mean for your understanding of the life and ministry of Jesus.

One exciting result of this book has been the development of an innovative drama in which a team of 15 Christians from a church or student group acts out every incident in the Gospel of Mark as theatre-in-the-round. The Mark Drama is now being performed in many countries around the world.

www.themarkdrama.com

ISBN 978-3-937965-21-5
Pb. • 106 pp. • £ 8.00

VTR Publications
info@vtr-online.com
http://www.vtr-online.com